Short-Term Therapy Techniques

by

Christ L. Zois, M.D.

Margaret Scarpa, M.A., C.S.W.

A Jason Aronson Book

ROWMAN & LITTLEFIELD PUBLISHERS, INC.

Lanham • Boulder • New York • Toronto • Oxford

A JASON ARONSON BOOK

ROWMAN & LITTLEFIELD PUBLISHERS, INC.

Published in the United States of America
by Rowman & Littlefield Publishers, Inc.
A wholly owned subsidiary of The Rowman & Littlefield Publishing Group, Inc.
4501 Forbes Boulevard, Suite 200, Lanham, Maryland 20706
www.rowmanlittlefield.com

PO Box 317
Oxford
OX2 9RU, UK

First Rowman & Littlefield edition 2004

British Library Cataloguing in Publication Information Available

Library of Congress Cataloging-in-Publication Data

Zois, Christ.
Short-term therapy techniques / by Christ L. Zois, Margaret Scarpa.
p. cm.
Includes bibliographical references and index.
ISBN: 978-0-7657-0026-1
1. Brief psychotherapy. I. Scarpa, Margaret. II. Title.
RC480.55.Z647 1997
616.89'14—dc20 96-26113

Printed in the United States of America

The paper used in this publication meets the minimum requirements of American National Standard for Information Sciences—Permanence of Paper for Printed Library Materials, ANSI/NISO Z39.48-1992.

To Wilhelm Reich, M.D.

whose work in *Character Analysis*

laid the foundation

for many of the principles

of insight-oriented, short-term therapy.

Contents

Foreword

What, you may ask, is the need for another textbook of short-term therapy? I venture to answer that this is truly a rare book in the vast literature of our craft. It is extremely readable, essentially free of psychiatric jargon, deceptively simple, yet very insightful and instructive for both the novice and the experienced therapist.

The authors have readily produced an excellent instructive manual on how to conduct a short-term psychotherapy. While Dr. Zois doesn't attempt to be encyclopedic, he is extremely practical and has not shied away from using in his vignettes extremely difficult patients who have been refractory to multiple prior insight-oriented therapies. For anyone who has experienced the hot seat of the therapist faced with angry or well-defended patients, it is truly revelatory and refreshing to observe a technical approach that penetrates through such defenses in a relatively short time, and the beneficial outcome of such interventions. I found it particularly instructive while reading his long vignettes to anticipate and compare what interventions I would have made to those chosen by Dr. Zois.

I am particularly grateful to Dr. Zois for his insights and discussions in two particular areas. One is his balanced approach to both the positive and negative feelings in the therapy. The other area involves his very original ideas on how, to some patients, the memory of the death of a loved one becomes the object relation rather than the individual. I found the latter discussion very perceptive and enlightening. Dr. Zois points out an obvious but often ignored issue: termination, saying goodbye, and loss can be as difficult for the therapist as the patient. The authors are obviously very well versed in the dynamics of the cases but are also not reluctant to bring a philosophical point of view to the analysis and interpretations.

I welcome this new edition to our library. I only wish that early in my training I had had such a text to guide me—certainly a lot of pain, on both sides, would have been spared.

Roosey Khawly, M.D.
New York City

Acknowledgments

To my publisher Jason Aronson, M. D., who invited me to write this work, for his support, encouragement and invaluable input. Also to Judy Cohen, Nancy D'Arrigo, and Norma Pomerantz of Jason Aronson Publishing, for making it all possible.

I am indebted to my colleagues and friends who read the manuscript and provided expert commentary: Michael Alpert, M.D.; Sonia Austrian, Ph.D.; Arlene Feinblatt, Ph.D.; Roosey Khawly, M.D.; John Moore, M.D.; and Carl Sonder, M.D.

To my son Elia Zois, who has worked with me over the years editing my presentation tapes and providing insight and moral support, for proofreading and editing this work.

Finally I am grateful to my co-author, Margaret Scarpa, whose clinical acumen and understanding of the dynamics of insight-oriented short-term therapy provided the structure for the text.

1

Short-Term Therapy: An Introduction

The necessity for an effective psychotherapeutic technique has been evident since Freud. Indeed STT (short-term therapy) operates within a general psychoanalytic framework. However, it utilizes techniques that work with the patient's defenses and resistance in a much more active way than the traditional approach. While founded on the same psychoanalytic principles as traditional therapies, short-term therapy is an active, challenging, focusing approach that utilizes techniques to exhaust the patient's defenses so that the patient experiences improvement as quickly as possible.

This book will demonstrate and explain the activity and techniques of STT by presenting a series of transcripts of actual therapies. Explanation of the therapist's thoughts and actions has been added to the transcripts.

Statements, interpretations, or questions that ST therapists commonly use are presented in italics.

ST therapy operates on the belief that, because core emotions are painful, patients who are allowed to be vague, to rationalize, or to intellectualize will avoid the very issues they need to confront. A traditional therapist is usually reluctant to challenge the defenses in the belief that a patient who avoids a topic is not comfortable enough to talk about it. Rather than seeing the avoidance or rationalization as an attempt to sabotage the therapeutic process, the therapist accepts the patient's defenses at face value. This amounts to a rationalization on the part of the therapist, that is, the patient "does not know the therapist well enough" to elaborate on an intimate or painful issue. A therapist who accepts a patient's statement at face value may suffer from similar conflicts. Such a therapist requires, at the least, self-analysis before he or she can become an effective agent for change.

Beginning with an evaluation that is both diagnostic and therapeutic, STT relies on the principle that the therapist stops gathering information whenever resistance arises and immediately challenges the defense. If the patient states that there is something he or she does not want to talk about, the therapist identifies the resistance and the need to sabotage the therapy. In *Character Analysis* (1953), Wilhelm Reich states, "Our principle is: No interpretation of meaning when a resistance interpretation is needed." He goes on to say, "If one interprets the meaning before eliminating the corresponding resistance the patient either accepts the interpretations for reasons of the transference, or he completely depreciates it . . . for experience shows that the therapeutic effect of the patient's communications is lost if they are made in the presence of unresolved resistances" (pp. 27–28).

After initial clarification of the patient's problem,

STT expedites the process of emotional change through constant challenge of the defenses. Rather than allowing the patient to be resistant, the therapist declares war on the defenses and breaks through them. Then, with the aid of the patient, the therapist uncovers the "loaded" emotional material that is at the core of the patient's conflicts.

The ST technique puts pressure on patients to commit themselves, to be clear, and, in a joint endeavor with the therapist, to take action and face the most painful, disconcerting, upsetting, and guilt-provoking issues in their lives.

The following are segments of a videotaped initial evaluation of a 37-year-old male. The evaluation is therapeutic as well as diagnostic.

Zois: Can you tell me what your problems are?

Alan: Yeah, what I know of them: Unable to communicate, no self esteem, unhappy.

Zois: What comes to your mind when you say you are unable to communicate?

Alan: I don't talk to people.

Zois: Who?

Alan: People in general.

Zois: But specifically?

Alan: Specifically?

Zois: Yes.

Alan: Everyone. I mean, people I work with, family.

Zois: When you say, "Everyone," that's very general. Who comes to your mind when you say you can't talk to people?

The standard opening question is asked, "Can you tell me what your problems are?" The patient attempts to use the defense of vagueness by generalizing. When I ask him to be specific he is put on notice that he will not be able to use his standard way of dealing with people, so he repeats my question, "Specifically?" He attempts to be general again by saying "Everyone." On a conscious and preconscious level he is already beginning to understand that he will have to acknowledge the issues he has been defending against all of his life.

Later in the evaluation we get to the subject of his ambivalence and self defeat.

Alan: On the other hand. . . .

Zois: There is another part of you that says you ought to continue in the old way?

Alan: That's right.

Zois: Is that familiar to you?

Alan: Yes, it is.

Zois: There's a part of you that wants to defeat what we do?

Alan: Yes, yes.

Zois: What comes to your mind when you say that?

Alan: In my work I have that part of me that is always in rare form, ready to go, ready to defeat myself.

Zois: Can you give me an example of that in your work?

Alan: Procrastination, not caring about my success, turning success into something negative.

Zois: How do you do that? Does an example come to your mind?

Alan: Yeah—I'm a designer. If I finish a very good job, I will never have it photographed. I will never have it published, which is an indication to me that I don't want to succeed, I don't want recognition.

Zois: So you've had thoughts about this?

Alan: Oh, yeah, yes.

Zois: So you actively put yourself in a beaten position at work?

Alan: Um-hmm.

Zois: Do you do it in other areas of your life?

Alan: Yeah, practically every area.

Zois: So you take a passive position?

Alan: Yeah.

Zois: Do you consider yourself a passive person?

Alan: No.

Zois: So on the one hand you put yourself in a beaten position, you are passive about your work, but in your mind you tell yourself you are not a passive person?

Alan: No.

Zois: What about that?

Alan: Because I've done stuff that has nothing to do with being passive. I mean, my work, my life has to do with being an achiever, being creative, which I do. I'm famous in my line of work. I'm respected.

Zois: So if you were to look at it, which is it? You tell me you don't have your work photographed, you don't allow yourself to gain attention in your work, but on the other hand you say that you are famous, you do achieve. So which is the point of view?

Alan: That I'm not famous. That I don't achieve.

Zois: So when you are telling me the other?

Alan: It's the reality, maybe.

Zois: You say "maybe."

Alan: Yes. I don't see it as a reality.

Zois: Do you find you sit on a fence on a lot of things?

Alan: All the time.

Zois: All the time?

Alan: Yes.

Zois: And are you on a fence here with me right now?

At this point in the session the patient is not highly resistant. He has only utilized the defense of vagueness: "maybe," "I think," "probably," and ambivalence.

He produces material when challenged. His anxiety level is not unusual, there is no interruption of cognitive function, that is, he has not reported that he has difficulty thinking or understanding under the pressure of my questions.

I move to the transference for the first time in terms

of his ambivalence and then to his emotion in the room with me.

Alan: Sure.

Zois: How do you feel right here with me now?

Alan: A little uncomfortable.

Zois: What comes to your mind?

Alan: I have a feeling of pressure in my chest.

Zois: How do you experience that pressure?

Always ask for the specific experience of an emotion in the transference and always ask for elaboration in the therapy in general.

Alan: It feels like a weight.

Zois: A weight. Where is it?

Alan: Right here and sometimes it comes up here [indicating].

Zois: What's the feeling that goes along with it?

Alan: Fear, anger.

Zois: So you are angry with me?

Alan: Yeah.

Zois: You are smiling.

Alan: Well, I shouldn't be angry with you, but I am.

Zois: You rationalize you shouldn't be, but you are.

Alan: Uh-huh.

Zois: As you tell me you are angry, as you declare it

to me you smile. Does your anger make you anxious?

Alan: Um-hmm.

Zois: How angry are you at the moment?

Alan: Angry enough to know I have a feeling of pain.

Zois: How angry is that?

Alan: Pretty angry.

Zois: What do you see in your mind?

Alan: That I would like to walk out of here.

Zois: So you would like to deal with your anger towards me with avoidance?

The patient is able to declare his anger with minimal challenge. He describes the defense of avoidance. I now attempt to link his anger in the transference to significant people in the past or present.

Alan: Correct.

Zois: Do you do that with other people?

Alan: Yes, mostly.

Zois: Who comes to mind?

Alan: This guy Dave that I work with. I avoid him because I'm angry at him most of the time.

Zois: When you think of being angry with him, what are you angry about?

Alan: It's probably not thinking that I'm serious about what I do. It's lack of support.

Zois: So he's not supportive of you?

Alan: No.

Zois: How angry do you become with him?

Alan: Angry enough to walk away.

Zois: What is the thought that causes you to walk away? How angry would you become before you would walk away?

This is a standard question to separate the defense avoidance from the emotion, anger. This is partly educative. People normally describe a defense when attempting to relate an emotion.

Alan: I want to strike out at him.

Zois: What do you picture in your mind when you say, "strike out at him."?

Alan: Just hit him across the face, a shot with my hand.

Zois: Where would you punch, with what?

Alan: My hand.

Zois: Your fist or your open hand?

Alan: Open hand.

Zois: Where would you punch him?

Alan: In the face.

Zois: Where?

Alan: Across the face.

Zois: Across the face?

Alan: Yes.

Zois: Where across the face?

Alan: On the cheek.

Although this line of questioning may appear tedious it is important to be as specific as possible. This serves two purposes: it facilitates placing the patient in the event being described, which makes the emotions more obvious to the patient and therefore easier to elicit, and it begins the process of desensitizing the ego to the angry impulses and homicidal fantasies. Overwhelming anger frequently causes a psychic paralysis. Therefore it is important to examine every aspect of the anger a patient experiences inside and outside of the transference.

Zois: On the cheek. What would happen to him if you did that?

Alan: It would probably devastate him.

Zois: What would happen to him in your mind when you see him?

Alan: He would fall apart, maybe cry.

Zois: He would start to cry?

Alan: Yes.

Zois: What would he look like?

Alan: Fairly pathetic, weak, stunned.

Zois: How do you feel as you think of him being pathetic and weak?

Constantly ask the patient the emotions he experiences as he describes what he sees in his mind. This is the beginning in the treatment of attempting to move the patient away from the anger/victim position to a more balanced view of his relationship with this man. I will do this with every relationship he introduces.

Alan: That he would never stick up for it.

He stays with the anger/victim role.

Zois: How do you feel as you think about it?

Alan: I feel angry.

Zois: As you see him weak and pathetic?

Alan: Yes.

Zois: How angry?

Alan: Very angry.

Zois: What do you see in your mind?

Alan: I see an image of him talking to me, talking about stuff that isn't supportive, where it should be.

Zois: You say you lash out at him in your mind, you strike him across the face and he looks weak and pathetic.

Alan: Yes.

Zois: What does his face look like?

Alan: Almost like a skeleton.

This description has implications for another significant person in his life.

Zois: What does that look like?

Alan: The character, I mean, it's all bare before you, the character is there.

Zois: What do his eyes look like?

Alan: They are green, bright green.

Zois: At that moment when you strike him.

Alan: There are no eyes. The eyes are closed.

Zois: So then you are saying that he is crying, he is stunned, he is weak and pathetic?

Alan: Yes.

Zois: How do you feel as you see him like that?

Alan: I feel angry and disgusted because I expected more, I wanted more. He is also a very old-time friend, a long friend.

There is some movement from the anger/victim position when he softens and acknowledges the friendship.

Zois: So you want him to be close?

I move quickly to introduce intimacy. Working on the intimacy and moving the patient to a balanced perspective of conflicted emotions contained within relationships is the key to a successful therapy.

Alan: Yes.

Zois: How do you feel that he's not?

Alan: I'm thinking maybe that the stuff I do, the stuff I've lived for, worked for, isn't necessary, isn't important, but yet he's there and I resent that.

Zois: So how do you feel that he's unfair to you, that he's not close to you?

Alan: He's there physically. He is not there emotionally.

Zois: How do you feel about that?

Alan: I feel angry about that. I feel like—I feel like it's almost a rape. It's almost a vandalism.

He retreats to anger/victim.

Zois: So how angry did you feel towards me?

Alan: Not that angry.

Zois: You are smiling again.

Alan: Yes.

Zois: How angry are you with me now?

Alan: Pretty angry.

Zois: So how angry?

Alan: Angry where I could slap you.

Zois: With your open hand?

Alan: Right.

Zois: Where would you slap me?

Alan: Across the face.

Zois: What would I look like if you slapped me across the face?

Alan: You would have a red mark on your face.

Zois: In your mind what would my reaction to you be?

Alan: I don't know.

Zois: When I ask you about your anger with me you become helpless. You say, "I don't know." What do you see in your mind? This is your thought, you are lashing out at me.

Alan: Probably one of numbness.

Zois: You say, "Probably." It's your thought. What would I be like?

I examine his anger in the transference. This makes him more anxious than his discussion of his anger toward his assistant. I challenge the vagueness and reassure him that his anger is only a thought in his mind. I will do this with his rage and homicidal fantasies also.

Alan: Numb, thinking that you would be used to it, it might have happened to you before, stunned, angry at me.

Zois: It makes you very anxious?

Alan: Yes.

Zois: When you become angry you become anxious and take a passive position?

I have now linked the three elements that constitute the triangle of emotions: (1) the impulse/feeling—anger, (2) the anxiety as a result of that anger, and (3) the defense of passivity to avoid the anxiety and anger.

Earlier he had described the defense of avoidance in reaction to his anger: "Angry enough to walk away."

Alan: Um-hmm, all the walls go up, the mechanisms.

Zois: You rationalize and you deal with it by avoidance?

Alan: Yes.

Zois: Now, you just took a deep sigh. *So there is still a wall between you and me?*

Alan: Probably, sure.

Zois: You say, "Sure." *If you keep that wall up then I'll be useless to you as with your associate. You won't allow me to get close to you.*

This is the standard approach to dealing with the patient's anxiety about intimacy and wish to sabotage therapy.

I also link two elements of the triangle of persons: the therapist and his associate from the present. I do not have information yet on people from the past.

Alan: It's about letting the wall down, right? But I don't know how to do it.

Zois: So you take a helpless position here?

Alan: Right.

Zois: You say, "Right," but your being right doesn't help us. So the question is, *"What are you going to do with your wall?"*

Alan: I'm going to try to tear it down if I can.

Zois: "Try, if I can"?

I challenge his defense of passivity.

Alan: Tear it down.

Zois: Do you have thoughts of lashing out at anybody else besides your associate and me?

Alan: No.

Zois: You never did? *Are you censoring yourself?*

When the patient makes a statement that obviously cannot be true, bring up the issue of censorship.

Alan: No, I'm trying. I'm trying to figure out if I ever have. No.

Zois: So you are saying throughout your life growing up and now as an adult you never had a thought of lashing out at anyone except your associate and me?

Alan: Not that I can remember.

Zois: So it's just the two of us?

Alan: At this point, yeah.

Zois: You smile.

Alan: I probably wanted to lash out at my brother.

Zois: You say, "probably"?

Alan: I did want to lash out at my brother.

Zois: You did want to?

Alan: Yes.

Zois: But you have some difficulty saying that to me.

Alan: Yes.

Zois: What comes to your mind?

Alan: That he was not a great brother and yet maybe deserved my anger or I should have been angry at him, but I couldn't be.

Zois: How old is your brother?

Alan: He's forty-two.

Zois: How old are you?

Alan: Thirty-seven.

Zois: What's your brother like?

Alan: He's not very much a man, not very much of a human being. He has cancer, a terrible form of cancer, which he's had for four years.

With minimal challenge I have easily and quickly hit paydirt. This is the reward of vigilance and eliciting specific information and elaboration.

Some of the psychodynamics of this case are now emerging: guilt because of sadistic/homicidal impulses toward a brother who is now dying, self-sabotage as a reaction to that guilt, and depression as a result of both.

Zois: What kind of cancer does he have?

Alan: Lymphatic.

Zois: How is he now?

Alan: He's okay. He's not okay. He's dying.

Zois: He's dying?

Alan: Yes. He's been—was in remission for three years, but slowly, I mean, he'll die.

Zois: What does he look like right now?

Alan: He looks very small and frail, birdlike.

Zois: What's his face like?

Alan: It's a caricature of itself.

Zois: What does that mean?

Alan: There is no substance there, just the form, just skin laying on bone, no personality, void of life.

Zois: So he's very thin?

Alan: Very, very thin, gaunt.

Zois: And his body?

Alan: Skeleton.

The description "skeleton" indicates the recapitulation of the anger toward his brother onto his assistant.

Zois: Where is he?

Alan: In Massachusetts.

Zois: When is the last time you spoke to him?

Alan: Spoken with him?

Zois: Spoken with him.

Alan: I've never spoken with him.

Zois: When is the last time you saw him?

I ignore his attempt to derail the conversation into a philosophical discussion about the lack of communication with his brother.

Alan: About a year ago.

Zois: What did he look like then?

Alan: The same.

Zois: The same?

Alan: Yes, as what I explained.

Zois: This is your image of him?

Alan: Yes.

Zois: Now, you say he is dying?

Alan: Yes.

Zois: Who does he live with in Massachusetts?

Alan: With my mother, she takes care of him.

Zois: How sick is he right now?

Alan: He's able to walk around, to eat, but he fails every day. I mean, every day he becomes weaker and there are some weeks when he has remission, but then the following week it gets a little worse.

Zois: Who tells you about his state right now?

Alan: My mom.

Zois: You talk to her?

Alan: Yeah.

Zois: You don't talk to him?

Alan: I'll speak with him when he's on the phone or when I call my mother he'll get on the phone and we'll talk.

Zois: When is the last time you talked to him?

Alan: When he was in the hospital.

Zois: What did he say to you?

Alan: He thanked me for making it possible for him to be in the hospital and taking care of him for years.

Zois: How do you feel about that?

Alan: I feel guilty about it.

Zois: You appear tearful.

Alan: Yeah, I am tearful.

Zois: Are you holding back those tears?

Alan: Yeah, a little.

Zois: You don't want to allow me to get close to you.

Always identify and interpret the transference implications of the patient holding back tears during therapy.

Alan: I do. I'm afraid.

Zois: You rationalize in your mind *you don't want me to be useful.* You are telling me your brother is useless to you all these years.

"You don't want me to be useful" is a phrase I will utilize time and again when working the intimacy in the transference.

I link the therapist and the past person, the brother, in my interpretation. The most effective interpretations involve the three elements of the triangle of persons—therapist, past, and present individuals. Here I should have included the assistant.

Alan: Um-hmm.

Zois: But we see here you have very mixed feelings about him.

I touch on the mixed feelings, this time with better result than my initial attempt with his emotions towards his assistant.

Alan: Yes, I do, because I love him dearly. I think, unfortunately, maybe his illness brought me to the realization, but I do love him dearly, but yet never wanted to.

He now easily speaks of his love for his brother and the conflict about it.

Zois: Have you ever declared that to him?

Always ask this question. It yields useful information on the patient's ability to experience intimacy. If the answer is negative in regard to someone who is dead it has implications for the degree of pathological mourning.

Alan: No, no.

Zois: So you are not prepared to say goodbye to him?

Alan: No, not yet.

Zois: You say, "Not yet"?

Alan: No. I think there are some things I have to talk to him about.

Zois: But you say you avoid him?

Alan: Yes.

Zois: So when that day comes to put him in his coffin and say your last goodbyes, he will be a voice from the grave?

This is a powerful image to evoke for the patient who has avoided coming to terms with relationships. If the person being discussed is already dead, phrase it in the present rather than the future: "So he is a voice from the grave for you."

Alan: It won't be resolved.

Zois: You see, you're telling me that you put off a lot of things in your life and that you're putting off declaring your feelings to your brother.

Alan: Yes.

Zois: So here again, you're attempting to put yourself in a position where you are a beaten man, that he will be dead for you and you will not have declared your feelings.

This is an interpretation of passivity and self sabotage.

Alan: Yes. It's not a very good feeling.

Zois: How do you feel right now?

Alan: I feel awful.

Zois: How do you experience that?

Alan: I feel drained right now, kind of fragmented.

Zois: What's the emotion?

Alan: A feeling of emptiness.

Zois: What's the emotion?

Alan: Fear.

Zois: So there is anxiety about getting in touch with your feelings?

Alan: Yes.

Zois: What's the feeling like here with me?

Alan: Angry.

Zois: So you want to use that anger to stay away from the pain?

Patients quickly learn your style. Here he attempts to use the idea of anger to divert me from the painful subject of his guilt and shame about his brother. I interpret the anger as a defense against pain rather than examine it as I had done earlier in the evaluation.

Alan: Yes.

Zois: You are going to try to ward me off with it. *You want to get back behind your wall?*

Alan: Yeah.

Zois: You don't want to keep *risking your neck here?*

I point out the anxiety that accompanies the idea of intimacy for him.

Alan: I do want—I don't want to risk it. I'm here, yet I don't want to risk it.

Zois: We see you're showing me your feelings, but there is another side of you that has the impulse to keep a wall—

It is important to acknowledge the progress the patient has made. If you do not do this you run the risk of being misperceived as punitive and accusatory in your questions.

Alan: Yes.

Zois: —and make me useless?

Alan: It's always easier to keep a wall.

Zois: You keep rationalizing about that, but you want to keep me useless and I'll be like your brother in your eyes, that you didn't allow him to get close to you, and now you say you have these thoughts since he's been ill that you love him.

I always put the interpretation in terms of the patient's impulses or behavior: "You didn't allow him to get close to you." To phrase it in terms of what his brother did to him is not the therapeutic issue. It only serves to support the victim role.

Alan: That one thought, that one time.

Zois: Now you want to minimize it?

I am pointing to his attempts to minimize the importance of his feelings for his brother.

Alan: No. I don't like to think about it.

Zois: So you avoid the thought?

Alan: Yes.

Zois: But in here you cry for him.

Alan: Yes.

Zois: What will you miss about him when he dies?

This is an important question. It forces the patient to explore his positive feelings. This man has spent his life angry with his brother, feeling victimized by him. Acknowledging his positive feelings toward his brother allows him to view the relationship in a more realistic light. It also brings him closer to abandoning the anger/victim role he has embraced in general.

Alan: He's my brother.

Zois: What will you miss about him?

Alan: Some memories that I have, a few fond memories as a child.

Zois: What are those?

Alan: After my father died he took the place of my dad.

Zois: How did he do that?

Alan: He was supportive.

Zois: In what way?

Alan: Brought me to school, met me after school.

Zois: How old were you?

Alan: I was ten. We were in the same school together. He would wait for me after school. We would kind of talk about what we were going to do, if I should go to work, if he should go to work to help support my mother and help support ourselves. That was maybe the only little part of me I ever saw in him, was that period of my life, but it meant something. I guess it meant that he cared.

Zois: You say, "I guess"?

Alan: Yeah. He never showed it any other way. He does care.

Zois: What comes to your mind when you say that?

Alan: The belief that he does. I see him smile.

Zois: When do you see that, when he smiles?

Alan: When I was a kid we played jokes, or would play a game and he would smile at it.

Zois: How would you feel when you would be there with him?

Alan: Okay, but they were very rare instances.

Zois: When did you have those memories of you and him, the time your father died, waiting for you after school, the two of you talking together?

Alan: I haven't.

Zois: When did they first come back to you?

Alan: Right now. It's great. I have some great memories playing with our dog. We had a crazy duck. The dog and the duck lived in the house together. It was a riot to play with them. He stood up for me in a fight once. I was having a fight with someone. He kept supporting me by egging me on. He was very supportive about it, made sure my bloody nose stopped bleeding. He got me home.

The patient reports that this is the first time he has recalled the positive aspects of his relationship with his brother. This supports short-term theory that challenge and focus will penetrate the defenses and result in the eliciting of productive material.

Zois: How old were you then?

Alan: I was about twelve.

Zois: In your mind, *when did things change*, your feelings towards him?

In the face of a relationship that changed it is important to examine when and how that change in attitude and feeling occurred. This will usually yield more information about the circumstances of the patient's life. Alan, for example, relates the significance of his father's death in terms of the impact it had on the family dynamics.

Alan: I think soon after my father's death I saw this kind of manipulating side of him. I spent a lot of time observing as a child. I would watch everything. To this day I watch and listen. I would see him setting things up.

Zois: What kind of things?

Alan: Situations that he would gain from.

Zois: Such as?

Alan: Such as wanting a car and doing everything he could to get a car.

Zois: To get a car from whom?

Alan: From my mother.

Zois: So he would set up situations that would involve your mother?

Alan: Right, and ultimately me, because I felt that—well, he got a car. I didn't get anything. But then he would get another car and another car.

Zois: And you?

Alan: Nothing, really.

Zois: So?

Alan: I didn't ask for it and I would have gotten it if I had asked. It was the manner in which he did it.

Zois: In your mind, *who was your mother closer to*, you or your brother?

When taking the history of siblings always ask, "In your mind who was your mother/father closer to?" This yields information relating to oedipal triangles.

Alan: My brother.

Zois: Who lived in the house with you, your mother and brother?

Alan: That's it.

Zois: Just the three of you?

Alan: Yes.

Zois: So as you saw it, it was the two of them and you?

Alan: Yes, but it was a very—I can't say that.

Zois: You're saying he got everything and you got nothing.

Alan: I got—I got—he had everything physically, monetarily. Maybe I got—

Zois: You say, "maybe."

Alan: Yeah, because I'm not sure.

Zois: So he got everything and you got nothing, or you got something too.

Alan: I got something too.

Zois: What?

Alan: I got a way of dealing with things, people.

Zois: That's very vague.

Alan: Yeah, of course it's vague.

Zois: You say, "of course."

Alan: Well, I'm vague.

Zois: Now you are back to vague, but we see you can be very specific. When I ask about you and your mother you become vague.

His vagueness indicates that the relationship with his mother is emotionally loaded.

Alan: I get emotional support from my mother in an unphysical way.

Zois: You say, "unphysical."

Alan: There was no embrace, not until very late, until maybe my thirties. There was some kind of act or interaction with one another. So as I look at it, it was a feeling that I wasn't getting anything because it wasn't how I would have liked it, how I would have wanted it to be.

Zois: In your mind, what did you want?

Alan: I wanted the feeling of security, someone putting an arm around me and saying, "Hey, it's okay."

Zois: Who was that someone?

Alan: It was my mother at that point.

Zois: How was she towards your brother then? Was she physical with him?

Alan: No. It's not in my mother's makeup. She was—all I can say was that he was getting physical rewards, you know, a car. I wasn't getting any of that. I felt sort of shortchanged.

We see how much material can be elicited and how much work can be accomplished in sixty minutes. This evaluation continued for another hour during which the relationship with his father and the death of his father were examined. I then covered his current and past intimate relationships, his sex life, including fantasies, and all the while I continued to focus and challenge the defenses whenever they arose.

This patient was only moderately resistant and was able to get in touch with underlying emotions with only gentle challenge on my part. He was able to show emotion in the room—tearfulness. These two elements allowed me to predict a successful outcome. A review of the degree of his sadistic impulses indicated they were not intense, as evidenced by the minimal resistance he mobilized. That also enabled me to conclude that the work could be accomplished in twenty-five to thirty sessions.

If you challenge and exhaust the defenses you will be rewarded with productive unconscious material. The converse is also true. If you do not challenge the defenses, the patient will become yet more defensive and no information or insights that are truly valuable to the patient will be generated.

Classic passive approaches to psychotherapy are

contrary to a systematic approach to problem solving. After an initial evaluation, the therapist takes steps to cure the patient's condition, using techniques that actively seek to solve the problem and take only as much time as is necessary.

This technique envisions the mapping out of a beginning, middle, and termination of therapy. After assessing the patient and developing a strategy for the treatment, the therapist applies a technique to overcome the patient's resistance and reach the patient's core issues, which the therapist and patient then work through until treatment is complete.

Will the change that takes place be permanent? Videotapes of follow-up sessions conducted one, three, and five years after the end of treatment demonstrate the efficacy of the ST technique. However, emotional health is an evolutionary process. The results of the process will continue as long as the patient works at it. If people do not remain vigilant about their emotions, attitudes, and behavior, the gains made in therapy will diminish as does physical fitness when diet and exercise are not maintained.

SIGNIFICANT FIGURES IN THE PATIENT'S LIFE: HOW TO DETERMINE WHICH ONES TO DEAL WITH AND IN WHAT ORDER

When you are doing the evaluation, you should examine all of the people that are significant to the patient. In order to make the choice of which individuals should be dealt with first and which later, it is necessary to first determine the intensity of emotions the patient attaches to each significant figure and then begin with the *least* emotionally charged individual. For example, if the patient has had a very intense, conflicted relationship with a sibling, that sibling should be dealt with later in the therapy. You must first desensitize the patient to anger and intense emotions. Conversely, if the patient states that he or she did not have any feelings about his or her father and that he or she cannot remember spending time with him, I consider that loaded emotional material that the patient has denied, repressed, and avoided. I would deal with the father after dealing with other less intense relationships.

THE TRIANGLES

As we saw in Alan's initial interview, the STT technique focuses on two important sets of forces, which can be visualized as two triangles. The first triangle is concerned with three categories of people who are significant in the patient's life: the present, the past, and the therapist. The second is the triangle of defense, anxiety, and impulse/feeling. The therapist may encounter the elements of these triangles in many different combinations.

The following vignette demonstrates how the therapist works with the triangles in employing the STT technique. The patient is angry at the therapist but the patient does not talk about it, and instead becomes tearful.

Zois: How do you feel right now?

Sue: I feel tearful.

Zois: What's the emotion under that tearfulness?

The patient experiences anger. However, her way of dealing with it involves defending against that impulse with weepiness.

Sue: I don't know.

Zois: "I don't know" is helplessness. What are you feeling?

Sue: Well, I'm a little angry at you.

Zois: A little angry?

Sue: I'm angry at you.

Zois: So when you get angry at me, you defend against it by becoming tearful. Who else did you treat that way?

Now I have touched on three points from the two triangles: the therapist, the impulse/feeling, and the defense.

Sue: My father.

Zois: Can you give me an illustration?

Sue: There was a time when he wouldn't let me use the family car and I got angry and burst into tears. I would always do that with my father.

Zois: How about in your current life?

After linking three points from two triangles—therapist, father, defense—I attempt to bring in a fourth.

Sue: My husband. He's always demanding, and I cry.

Zois: When you cry, how are you really feeling?

Sue: Angry.

I have effectively utilized nearly all the points on the two triangles—the therapist, a person from the past, a person from the patient's current life, a defense, and an impulse/feeling—to bring the patient to the point where she can see how she has masked her emotions with a defense and how that defense is used and perpetuates itself.

THE ROLE OF THE DEMONSTRABLE TECHNIQUE/THE USE OF THE VIDEO CAMERA

The only way to bring about change in psychotherapeutic concepts and attitudes is to have the ability to demonstrate that a technique is effective. Videotape technology has made this possible. Therapists can now create a record of the application of such a technique and of the patient's response. This not only validates, it affords a means of studying and refining concepts.

Instead of relying on esoteric theories to explain behavior, the therapist should observe the results of therapeutic interactions and craft a technique based on those observations. The video camera has done for psychotherapy what the electron microscope has done for biology. It has brought therapy into the modern world.

Videotaping has played an important historical role in the development of the demonstrable technique of STT. Tapes of actual sessions are essential tools for the learning and honing of skills, on the part of both students of therapy and experienced professionals. Moreover, videotaping allows accountability in what has been a very inexact science.

I want to stress that I am speaking only of the need

for therapists to share the data recorded in sessions with their colleagues. In no way do I advocate the dissemination of information about patients in any other quarter. Patients who allow their sessions to be videotaped are aware that the tapes will be used for training and research purposes.

Before videotape technology was available, it was difficult to create useful records of therapy sessions. Handwritten notes are subjective and depend on how much the therapist can remember. Audio recording is a poor substitute for the audiovisual image of patient and therapist.

Videotaping allows for careful scrutiny of the therapeutic process, where not only the spoken word but the mannerisms and the facial expressions of both patient and therapist can be documented. Therapists can study in detail how they and other therapists have conducted sessions, and the technique can continuously evolve. Videotaping sessions makes the ST technique a uniquely demonstrable one that validates or invalidates any theory and allows that theory to be refined.

The material that the patient provides sometimes validates hypotheses, and other times demands modification of what formerly was sacrosanct psychoanalytic dogma. For example, Freud emphasized sexual and aggressive impulses as the key elements in what he referred to as the unconscious. When we study videotapes of patient's responses to focused questioning, we see that they struggle with other feelings as well—pain, grief, sadness, guilt—and that these issues are as important as aggression and sexuality, if not more so. Most of the information presented in this book is derived from insights gained during almost twenty-five years of studying the videotaped therapy sessions of hundreds of patients.

THE VALUE OF VIDEOTAPING FOR THE THERAPIST

Videotapes have their greatest value, however, when the therapist can review his or her own sessions with patients. Through reviewing tapes of sessions I have gained tremendous information and insight as to how I might improve my technique. Throughout my career, videotapes have helped me to identify areas that I mistakenly believed I had dealt with correctly or issues that I had missed. Beyond that, they have allowed me to understand how I might have handled sessions differently and more effectively. Dr. Michael Alpert of St. Clair's Hospital observed in a recent article (1996), "In the end, therapists as well as patients gain from videotaping the patient–therapist interaction. Supervisors, peers, and even patients have pointed out my misunderstandings and distortions. . . . I have had the experience in self-supervision of looking back at a session and seeing that events were not as I remembered. Sometimes I did not hear the patient. Sometimes I missed nonverbal communications; other times I misunderstood the patient" (p. 102).

Another wonderful benefit of videotaping was that it finally documented that if the therapist challenges the defense and does not ignore it, the patient becomes less defensive. In fact, if the therapist does not challenge the defense and does ignore it, the patient will become more defensive and the therapy will be at risk. This was the reverse of the conventional wisdom, which said that it is dangerous to probe for the patient's strong feelings. Videotaping documents instead that, when challenged, patients improved.

Within the therapeutic community, there has been a great deal of resistance to videotaping. There may be several reasons why therapists would be unwilling to show their work. One might be that a therapist does not have faith in his or her work, or even has a problem with his or her sense of self. A second issue might be the danger of exposing oneself to the criticism of others.

The other criticism is that it's intrusive, that the patient is distracted by the camera. In the thousands of hours that I have videotaped, I can recall only two instances where a patient even looked directly at the camera. I have never had a patient comment on the intrusiveness of the camera or a sense of feeling uncomfortable. It has been my experience, both in the therapies I have conducted and in videotaped therapies I have observed, that the patient's discomfort with the camera is directly proportional to the therapist's discomfort with the camera. If the therapist is uncomfortable with the camera being in the room, there is a high degree of probability that the patient will pick this up and sense that same discomfort. However, if the therapist is comfortable with the philosophy behind the concept of videotaping, this acceptance will become part of the covert dialogue with the patient.

I have dealt with the camera by not making much of it in an analytic sense. Before coming into the therapy room the patient signs a release that states that the video camera will be used. The release explains that the tapes are for my own use. If the patient agrees, the tapes could also possibly be used to share information with other mental health professionals in conferences or in small groups. The patient has the final say as to whether that can or cannot be done. The patient also gives or withholds permission to use segments of the videotapes for publication in articles or books. When the patient enters the room, the tape is already running.

Without a demonstrable technique, there can be no

effective therapy. Therapists are not artists. The artist can intuit what the therapist cannot. Therapists must systematically observe and refine their information, and that cannot be done by referring to notes made after the session. Reports from therapists who do not audio or video record are similar to what Plato spoke of in his allegory of the cave: shadows on the wall.

THE IMPORTANCE OF DEMYSTIFYING THE THERAPEUTIC PROCESS

Psychotherapy is burdened by a kind of mystique, a belief that the therapist is omnipotent. This mystique presents dangers for the therapeutic process, since it fosters passivity.

Therapists tend to keep a certain distance from their patients, for a variety of reasons. One is an attempt—conscious or unconscious—to lessen the anxiety that arises from a belief in their omnipotence. Another reason may be a reluctance to probe areas that are painful for the therapist as well as the patient. Distance between therapist and patients tends to support the mystique of therapy. However, the mystique is generated primarily by the patient's own transference and neurotic needs—the need to be taken care of and the need to believe that the therapist is omniscient and therefore there will be a positive result. Many of my patients have viewed segments of tapes of their evaluation and sessions. They have then told me how valuable it was to see themselves as they were at that time. Encouraging the patient to view the videotapes of their sessions is one of the most effective ways to demystify the process. The patient is able to see much more clearly how their attitudes and statements color the therapeutic relationship after such reviews.

NOURISHING THE NEUROTIC PROCESS

Another aspect of the mystique of therapy is the belief that what is said in the therapy room is for the therapist's ears alone. In terms of confidentiality vis-à-vis the outside world, that is certainly appropriate. However, even with appropriate confidentiality there is an unspoken nourishment of the neurotic process (the patient's need to hold on to inappropriate feelings and attitudes), because the excessive privacy of therapy reinforces the patient's belief that what he or she is saying is in some way terrible, so terrible that only this "omniscient" and "omnipotent" father or mother figure or confessor can be the repository of those "confessions." That sense of singularity about one's thoughts, attitudes, and fantasies is most conducive to increasing the neurotic view.

DEFUSING THE NEUROTIC PROCESS

The neurotic process can be defused when the patient understands that his or her thoughts are universal, that he or she has a connection with other people who have had similar thoughts and fantasies and similar struggles in dealing with them. However, this cannot happen if the therapist does not take steps to demystify the therapeutic process.

A person may have upsetting thoughts: wishes that a parent would die, sexual fantasies, or homicidal impulses. Sometimes we consider ourselves freaks, sadistic maniacs, even potential murderers because of these thoughts. On a less dramatic level, we are often reluctant to talk to others about feelings of inadequacy, anger, or guilt. We may even have trouble admitting such feelings to ourselves.

Because the confidentiality that is part of traditional therapies can encourage patients to believe that the feelings discussed in therapy are shameful, the videotaping that is done for purposes of documentation functions as a therapeutic tool as well. It cuts against the grain of the patient's neurotic guilt—the notion that the matters discussed in therapy are terrible and should be hidden from others.

CANDIDATES FOR STT

STT is not for people with significant cognitive impairment, who are unable to function because their view of the world has been distorted by severe mental illness. It is not for psychotic people who have had to use medications or have been institutionalized for treatment. STT is for people who are able to experience aspects of themselves that they ordinarily might not acknowledge. Patients must be able to tolerate painful material from the past that they tended to diminish or ignore. STT poses no dangers for those people who fall into the neurotic category. These people may be in pain, but they operate within a realistic set of notions about themselves in relation to the outside world.

2

The Therapist

ELEMENTS OF AN EFFECTIVE THERAPIST

In order for the therapy to benefit the patient, the therapist must bring to the psychodynamic process the ability to tolerate patients' worst fears, emotions, and beliefs about themselves. That ability is sometimes taken for granted, but should not be. Secondly, the therapist must have a technique for dealing with the outward manifestations of the psychodynamic process of the patient. Without that technique, it will be difficult, if not impossible, for the therapist to get past the resistances and defenses of the patient.

Therapists can be active, passive, or advice-giving. ST therapists actively interact with the patient. In order to be effective a ST therapist must have mastered three areas:

- The interaction with the patient—the transference and countertransference.
- The monitoring of the patient's psychodynamics.
- The application of the STT technique.

STT differs from a passive approach because not only is understanding the psychodynamics important but the technically effective statement or question must be at the therapist's fingertips.

THE ABILITY TO TOLERATE THE PATIENT'S AND YOUR OWN EMOTIONS: ANXIETY, ANGER, GUILT

When a patient is telling you his or her life story, the patient will experience a variety of emotions—anxiety, anger, guilt, grief. As you interact and intervene to focus on those issues, you must be aware that what the patient is relating can affect you. The anxiety, guilt, or anger generated by the patient can resonate with your own emotions. A patient's tearful account of the last time he or she saw a parent alive may make you remember a similar event in your life. In order to be effective in making the correct intervention, you have to recognize that similar emotional elements may be at play in you, the therapist.

Patients attempt to avoid painful material. The therapist can also suffer from the same malady. When the patient starts to talk about an issue that is painful for the therapist, the therapist's initial reaction may be to avoid that issue.

THE ABILITY TO TOLERATE INTIMACY

One definition of intimacy is the ability to allow someone to be useful to you. In therapy, your usefulness is directly proportional to how close you allow the patient to come to you, and how close you can be to the patient. This closeness is accomplished by sharing the information the patient has offered and the emotions and the pain he or she may be experiencing.

Empathy is an essential part of intimacy. One of the hallmarks of an effective therapist is the ability to communicate to the patient, both overtly and covertly, that you appreciate his or her pain and that you have empathy for that pain. This is not to say that you feel that pain. You do not want to become a fellow mourner, or someone who only sympathizes. The therapist has to communicate he is prepared to take this journey through whatever uncharted areas of pain, shame, grief, and anger that the patient has to traverse. If the therapist has anxiety about those issues, the patient will not feel supported in the effort, which will be a complication and an obstacle to a successful outcome. Too often therapists who have problems in these areas end up intellectualizing and giving advice to the patient. The therapy then deteriorates into a support session where the patient comes in and expects to be told what to do. Accomplishing intimacy is essential to any successful therapeutic result.

DIFFERENTIATING BETWEEN TRANSFERENCE AND THE PATIENT'S GENUINE POSITIVE FEELINGS

It is important to appreciate that the patient generates two sets of feelings towards the therapist. The first area is well known and much discussed—the transferential feelings. The other, which is less often acknowledged, is the patient's genuine feelings toward a therapist for having helped. Frequently, positive feelings make the patient anxious because these tender feelings are confused with sexual feelings. This is common in both men and women. The therapist should be on the alert when dealing with these emotions, especially with a patient of the same sex. In that situation, the anxiety can be much greater because the patient has fears that the emotions have some homoerotic basis. The confusion of tender feelings with sexual feelings has its etiology in several areas. One is the belief throughout their lives that when they are in a relationship just being friends or just providing companionship is not enough, that they have to provide something more of themselves and that something more is sex. This prejudiced point of view is brought into the therapy. When a patient feels helped and tender feelings are generated, sexual feelings frequently manifest themselves. It is important however to understand that these are not really sexual feelings. They are tender feelings and the patient is responding in a familiar way to the therapist just as he or she has responded to other people throughout his or her life. For example, the patient who reports, two-thirds of the way through a successful therapy, with some embarrassment:

Luanne: I had a dream about you last night.

Zois: What was the dream?

Luanne: I had a dream we were making love.

I do not ask for elaboration at this point because it can be confusing to the patient.

Zois: How did you feel when we were making love?

Luanne: I felt good.

I immediately go to the interpretation.

Zois: So you have tender feelings towards me.

Luanne: Yes.

Zois: As you think about those tender feelings what comes to your mind?

Luanne: You have been there for me through these months.

Zois: We see then when you have tender feelings they become associated with sexual feelings. Have you done that before in your life?

Luanne: Yes.

Zois: What comes to your mind?

Luanne: When I was working in this company the man who was my supervisor would visit my division on a weekly basis and he was always very good to me. When I first started working there I easily could have gotten fired but he helped me very much and the relationship became sexual in that he would come to my office and I would perform oral sex on him most of the times he'd visit.

Zois: What are your thoughts on that?

Luanne: Well, as I look at it now it really wasn't the sex but I just didn't know what else to do for him to show my appreciation.

Zois: What do you think about that now as you look at it?

Luanne: Looking back at it I think it's pretty silly, but at the time it seemed the thing to do.

Zois: Do any other examples come to your mind?

Luanne: When I was a teenager and I wanted boys to like me.

HOW TO AVOID THE EMERGENCE OF THE NEUROTIC TRANSFERENCE, EVEN IN THE BRIEFEST SHORT-TERM THERAPIES

The only way to avoid the neurotic transference is to constantly examine transferential material. That involves working on the intimacy in the transference. The patient has to experience in the room the emotions generated by the therapist's questioning and challenging. As we have discussed before, one of those emotions is anger at the therapist for stirring up feelings and penetrating into the patient's life. The examination of the impulse component of the defense in the transference is one of the major curative factors in the therapy. If this is not done the patient will form a neurotic attachment to the therapist. The therapist cannot help the patient be free from other neurotic attachments if the relationship with the therapist is no different. Working through the neurotic transference is the key to resolving the conflicted relationships in the person's life and bringing about a successful termination.

IMPLICATIONS OF LOSS

The ability to deal with loss is one of the universal challenges in life. Patients often do not want therapy to end, just as they have not wanted to give up attachments to other significant figures. However, if the therapist has applied the technique effectively, has consistently challenged and focused on the patient's resistance, has examined the patient's emotions with significant people, has dealt with the issue of intimacy and usefulness between patient and therapist, and has scrutinized both the transference and the patient's genuine feelings toward the therapist, then saying goodbye will not be a stumbling block to termination.

3

Elements of the Short-Term Therapy Technique

A therapeutic resolution occurs when the therapist is successful in implementing six major elements of the ST therapy technique.

- Clarifying of feelings and issues
- Challenging the defenses
- Closing the gap between thought and feeling
- Reaching buried emotions
- Achieving emotional balance
- Moving toward intimacy

The sections that follow will discuss these elements and show, through a transcript of a therapy session, how the therapist works with each element. In STT, no question or dialogue is superfluous; everything is geared toward accomplishing an end.

CLARIFICATION OF FEELINGS AND ISSUES

An effective therapy elicits clarity. Most people who enter treatment are vague about their problems. This difficulty is compounded by the ambiguity of everyday language: we all use the words "maybe," "perhaps," "I think," "I guess." Outside of therapy, this vagueness is tolerated and not questioned. As a result, most patients initially have difficulty describing their thoughts and feelings accurately.

ST technique does not permit vagueness, which is one of the most common defenses. In a methodical way, patients must commit and assert themselves. The therapist who tolerates vagueness is not going to help patients understand their problems; in allowing vagueness to pass unchallenged the therapist actually encourages a lack of progress.

The therapist must address a lack of clarity every time it occurs, until the patient becomes aware of the need to be clear and committed in every statement made. "I think I am angry" is not acceptable. The patient either is angry or is not angry, and must make a clear statement about whichever is the case.

The following transcript is taken from an evaluation of a woman who came to therapy stating that she was having problems in her marriage.

Zois: Does he say that you want things to be your way in the relationship between you and him?

Jamie: Yeah, I guess so.

Zois: You say you guess so. Is it yes or no?

Jamie: A little bit, yeah.

Zois: You say a little bit. So *you don't want to commit yourself.*

Jamie: Yeah, I think so.

Zois: You say "I think" again.

Jamie: Yeah.

Zois: Do you have difficulty asserting yourself?

Jamie: Not usually.

Zois: *Do you consider yourself a passive person?*

Jamie: In some ways.

Zois: You say "In some ways." That's a passive statement. Are you or aren't you?

Jamie: I don't think that things are black and white.

Zois: Now you intellectualize.

Jamie: I'm here for the first time.

Zois: Now you want to rationalize why you can't commit.

Jamie: I don't know.

Zois: So you're helpless. You say "I don't know." What will happen if you remain passive and helpless here?

Jamie: Then I will fail.

Zois: What do you want to do about that?

Jamie: What can I?

Zois: Do you notice when I make an interpretation you become passive? You ask me a passive question, "What can I do?"

In this vignette we see the patient mobilize many defenses: helplessness, rationalization, intellectualization, and vagueness. This is not uncommon. The important issue here is that the therapist challenges each one.

CHALLENGING THE DEFENSES

In the face of resistance, any exchange of information between patient and therapist is meaningless. Even the most motivated patients come to treatment with some degree of resistance. Therefore, challenging it is a recurring component of every therapy. Resistance manifests itself as a series of defenses, which vary from person to person.

The ST technique cuts through the smoke screen of defenses the individual uses to obscure issues. The therapist challenges defenses until they are exhausted. It is a straightforward situation: if the patient is not answering the question, he or she is being defensive. As the therapist, you must challenge defenses immediately; there is nothing to be gained by waiting.

The challenge to the patient's defenses may arouse anger on the part of the patient. By not allowing the patient to use his or her customary defenses, the therapist threatens to expose the patient to the painful feelings he or she has been trying to avoid.

The therapist's questions also generate anxiety. The patient sees that the therapist is attempting to get close emotionally, and the patient's anxiety increases because of the conflicts that intimacy can trigger. As the therapist persists, however, the patient's defenses are exhausted, and he or she feels relief as the blocked feelings are liberated. The challenge to the defenses is the first step toward intimacy between therapist and patient.

Defenses are often ingrained habits that are eradicated only with repeated effort. In challenging the defenses, repetition is important. The patient may see that an attitude is defensive and thus may have an insight about his or her behavior and feelings, but that does not mean the defense goes away immediately or that the insight stays with the patient from that time onward.

Continuing Jamie's evaluation, I find she is reluctant to discuss an affair she is having.

Zois: When did you begin this affair?

Jamie: Two months ago.

Zois: How do you know this man?

Jamie: I just do.

Zois: How do you know him?

Jamie: Do I have to say?

Zois: Do you have to say?

Jamie: Do I have to tell you?

Zois: You want to keep me out of your life. You don't want me to get close to you. You want to keep a wall between us.

Jamie: I'd much rather not.

Zois: So if you don't tell me—

Jamie: Is it important, how I met him, what his profession is?

Zois: What?

Jamie: He's a doctor.

Zois: What kind of doctor?

Jamie: He's not a psychiatrist or anything like that.

Zois: What's the problem telling me about it?

Jamie: I don't know.

Zois: Did you censor yourself in the other therapy that you were in?

Jamie: Yes.

Zois: Were there things in the other therapy that you didn't want to talk about?

Jamie: Yes.

Zois: So you sabotaged that therapy.

When discussing a patient's prior therapy it is important not to be critical of that therapist or attempt to evaluate his skills but rather view the issue from the perspective of the patient sabotaging the prior therapy.

Jamie: I never thought of it that way.

Zois: There is some difficulty in telling me about this person?

Jamie: Yes, could we talk about how I feel instead?

Zois: But there is a problem that you're having in being open with me. Do you have that problem with other people?

Jamie: Yes, I do.

Zois: Do you keep people at a distance?

Jamie: Yes.

If after repeated attempts the patient refuses to divulge information then I shift technically to the interpretation of self-sabotage.

Zois: If you continue to keep a wall between us I will be useless to you. Then what will happen to the therapy?

Jamie: It will fail.

Zois: I can afford to fail. However, you will leave here with your suffering intact. *Why do you want to do this to yourself?*

"I can afford to fail" tells the patient I am not omnipotent. "Why do you want to do this to yourself" is an appeal to the unconscious.

The following vignette is another example of how a patient attempts to censor and distance herself from the therapist.

Zois: Your thought is what it would be like to have sex with your supervisor?

Diana: Yes.

Zois: What did you picture in your mind?

Diana: I didn't. I mean, I just didn't.

Zois: As you look at it now?

Diana: I don't want to picture it.

Zois: You are having trouble letting me into your intimate thoughts?

Diana: Yeah, yeah.

Zois: What are we going to do about that?

Diana: I don't know. It's so embarrassing.

Zois: You're talking about "embarrassing." *You are trying to keep a distance from me.*

Diana: Yeah.

Zois: What?

Diana: Yes.

Zois: What do you picture in your mind?

Diana: I don't know.

Zois: You are retreating.

Diana: I can't. No, I can't.

Zois: Again, it's "I can't," with the passivity and helplessness.

Diana: Okay. I don't want to.

Zois: And defenses and "I don't want to" as a defense against allowing me into your life, into your intimate thoughts, which is what you have been doing to yourself all your life, not letting anybody in. Do you want to continue that way?

Diana: No.

Zois: What are we going to do here? We see there is a part of you that wants to go on in the old way denying, rationalizing.

Diana: No. It's just embarrassing, that's all.

Zois: You rationalize some more as to why you can't allow me to be close to you.

Diana: I did tell you about it.

Zois: The issue is allowing me to be close to you.

Diana: Yeah.

Zois: So?

Diana: Yeah.

Zois: What do you want to do about that? Do you want to continue staying behind your wall and going through life like that?

Diana: No.

Again, an interpretation. We see that the level of defensiveness in the transference to material laden with guilt and shame rises precipitously. As we go on, she tries hard to keep up a wall. The degree of resistance has to do with transferential issues in terms of her impulses toward early significant people in her life.

Zois: What do you want to do about that? You tell me you've had these thoughts.

Diana: I want to tell you about that but it's too soon.

Zois: Too soon is a rationalization.

Diana: You want to jump at it.

Zois: It's a rationalization for maintaining your distance.

Diana: I know. Yes, that's part of it.

Zois: What's part of it?

Diana: Maintaining that distance.

Zois: You want to continue to do that to yourself?

Diana: No.

Zois: Well?

Diana: But I just can't.

Zois: What do you want to do here? See, you are back to "I can't," but we see here that you have the information. You want to take a helpless position and keep a distance and say, "I can't." We are in a situation now where you do know the answer. You see, it's not whether you know the answer or not, it's the question of the closeness here and the intimacy. What do you want to do about that?

CLOSING THE GAP BETWEEN THOUGHT AND EMOTIONS

On one end of the spectrum are those who are aware of their feelings, are not intimidated by them, and are able to declare them. As a result they usually do not experience a sense of paralysis in their lives and do not have many intense conflicts. Such people recognize the difference between an emotion and a defense. They do not say, "I was so angry I cried," or, "I was so angry I left the room." They have no trouble expressing how they feel about the therapist and other people. A therapist can evaluate these patients and determine within ten or fifteen minutes that they are in touch with their emotions.

Other people readily use defenses but are quick to learn not to. The therapist helps educate them about the difference between a defense and an emotion. These patients understand rather easily and by the end of the evaluation have changed some of their ways of responding. They no longer say "maybe," "I think," "I guess," and they take this new sense of clarity away with them.

At the far end of the spectrum are those people who are in isolation, meaning that their thoughts and feelings are not synchronous but operate on tracks that are far apart. Rather than admit irritation because of criticism leveled at them at work, they might say that the boss has been under a lot of stress. Such people often do not know what an emotion is. The result is emotional paralysis and, very likely, a failure to find success or contentment in life.

By pressuring, challenging, and focusing, the therapist enables these emotionally isolated patients to bring their thoughts and feelings together: "What do you mean?" "You're describing what you did, not what you felt." "What is your emotion?" The therapist keeps these patients boxed in and stays right on top of them so that they are up against the ropes. Finally, their emotion emerges.

Therapists can allow less defensive individuals more latitude. If constant pressure is not applied with highly resistant people, they will inevitably slip away into their defenses.

At this point in Jamie's session she is discussing a previous therapist.

Zois: You have the feeling that he doesn't care. Isn't that the thought you had?

Jamie: Yes.

Zois: How did you feel about that?

Jamie: Nothing. I didn't feel anything.

Zois: Let's look at that.

Jamie: He's just a therapist.

Zois: Now you make him "just a therapist." You rationalize. Before you wanted him to care.

Jamie: Of course I want people to care.

Zois: See how you defend against hurtful feelings. You generalize about "people." We are talking about your prior therapist.

Jamie: If you know, then why do you ask me?

Zois: Now you're irritated with me that I make you look at them.

Jamie: You don't irritate me.

Zois: You said you were irritated before. Do you have trouble with your anger?

Jamie: Oh, I don't know anymore. Maybe I do.

Zois: You notice you're becoming vague?

Jamie: I don't know if I have a problem with my anger.

Zois: A minute ago you were irritated with me, then you were uncomfortable telling me so when I asked you.

Jamie: The reason I'm irritated is if I knew all of the answers I wouldn't be here.

Zois: You have difficulty saying you're irritated with me.

Jamie: Because I'm not positive. I don't know what I feel.

Zois: You're ambivalent. You sit on the fence. Do

you have trouble showing your anger to anyone else?

Jamie: Yes.

The patient with coordinated thought and emotions has a much shorter road to travel. The therapy will require fewer sessions than the person whose cognition and emotions are out of sync. The isolated individual will require much more work. Isolation indicates that there are intense emotions underlying the highly defended psyche. Intense rage, guilt, sadness, or grief is responsible for the inability to bring emotions to a conscious level. That is the operating formula: emotional paralysis equals intense hidden feelings. Awareness equals less pathological material.

The ease or difficulty in focusing on and dealing with the defenses is an important diagnostic indicator. The man who is comfortable telling me that he is angry with me is a *symptom neurotic*; he is relatively easy to treat. The one who has no idea of what he is feeling is an *obsessive character disorder*; his treatment requires more work and will take longer (up to 35 or 40 sessions), because he is walled off from his emotions. His treatment will take longer because it is going to require constant work on his many defenses to get through them to underlying emotions. The symptom neurotic utilizes fewer defenses; he is in touch with his feelings and therefore capable of understanding the psychodynamic linkage that the therapist makes for him.

If you ask a patient, "How are you feeling?" and she replies, "I'm sad" or "I'm happy" or "I feel angry," she is in sync with her emotions. If she replies with a defense, such as a response that indicates helplessness, she is not in sync with her feelings. The first person is able to identify feelings and therefore able to examine them and integrate them into the psychodynamic issues.

In the following vignette the two modes are explored. For this man, the cognitive and the emotional parts of his psyche are out of sync.

Zois: How do you feel that I'm asking you questions about the first time you had sex with your wife?

George: I don't know.

Zois: What's the feeling?

George: I don't know what you're talking about.

I ask another man the same question.

Zois: How do you feel that I'm asking you questions about your wife?

Richard: I think it's none of your business.

Zois: What's the emotion that goes with that?

Richard: I'm angry at you.

REACHING BURIED EMOTIONS

There is within each person a psychic engine driven in part by intense feelings of anger, pain, and guilt. People hide these feelings from the world because they perceive them to be too dangerous to acknowledge. In the process, they hide them from themselves.

People are often ashamed or fearful when they have strong negative emotions. Such feelings make them uncomfortable, as do the memories of what caused the feelings and the impulses to which they give rise. As a result, these people live with the false idea that if you do not think about something it must not be there.

As the therapist challenges and exhausts the patient's defenses, the patient faces his or her strongest emotions and can begin to resolve such problems as self-sabotage, loneliness, and a host of interpersonal issues.

The following is a excerpt from the transcript of a patient whose entire evaluation will be examined later. Here he is discussing his father's death.

Zois: Did you see him after he was dead in the hospital?

Dean: Yes.

Zois: What did he look like?

Dean: I don't know—dead.

Zois: What was that like?

Dean: Now I'm angry because you're messing around in areas that I don't want you to be in.

Zois: So to this day you still can't look at it. You've never really said goodbye to him?

Here I move away from the anger to deal with the issue of his never saying goodbye to his father. This is a turning point in the therapy.

Dean: No.

Zois: Where was he? Was he lying in the bed?

Dean: Yes.

Zois: Was he on his back?

Dean: Yes.

Zois: What did he look like?

Dean: I don't know.

Zois: What was the color of his skin?

Here it is important to put him in the room with his father.

Dean: Ash. I don't know if he still had all of the tubes in him. I just don't know.

Zois: Was anybody else in the room?

Dean: I don't think so.

Zois: How do you feel now as we look back on it?

Dean: Scary. The wall works for me, doesn't it?

Zois: You were in the room alone with him?

Dean: You didn't answer my question. I use the wall against myself as well as against other people.

Zois: You're asking me now. Are you leaving the room with your father?

I do not become diverted despite the patient's attempts. I keep the patient in the room with his father. Even though his observations or anxiety about intimacy are valid I leave that issue for another time. Patients often attempt to derail the line of inquiry by offering material that is tempting to pursue.

Dean: No. I see what I'm doing. I see that.

Zois: Let's look at him now. He's in that room with you now alone. He's ashen?

Dean: He's lying on his back.

Zois: Is it the intensive care unit or a hospital room?

Dean: A private room. I feel tremendous anger right now. He died and left me with my mother.

Zois: When did you have that thought?

Dean: Just now.

The patient is now producing under pressure.

Zois: How were you feeling in the room with him?

Dean: Sad.

Zois: What did you do when you were there?

Dean: I touched him, I think.

Zois: Where?

Dean: His hands, his face.

Zois: What did that feel like?

Dean: I don't know but I'm feeling pretty sad right now.

You see how an initially resistant patient begins to produce valuable material. Interpreting anger as a defense in the transference allows Dean to bring to the surface the underlying sadness. The process of bringing the feeling to the surface moves the patient to a more balanced view of once conflicted attitudes.

ACHIEVING EMOTIONAL BALANCE

Therapists strive to help patients achieve the balance of feelings that exist in all relationships. Eliciting positive feelings that previously were obscured by overwhelmingly negative ones can help release a patient from anger or a sense of pain and victimization that has dominated his or her life. It can free the patient from the guilt that strangles his or her ability to live with satisfaction and a sense of harmony with the world.

Many people who come to therapy are able to focus only on their anger or their sense of being cheated or victimized. They push aside the tender feelings that coexist with the stronger painful ones. Sometimes those tender feelings are pushed beyond recall.

The therapist helps the patient move from static anger or sense of victimization to a more dynamic acknowledgment of tender feelings. Acknowledging both sets of feelings serves to lessen the paralysis engendered when strong negative emotions dominate our lives. The patient's anger, for instance, does not go away, but it becomes balanced with tenderness. The acknowledgment of ambivalence then leads to successful resolution of conflicted feelings.

In addition to anger and a sense of victimization, guilt can result in a belief of lack of entitlement. This is illustrated by the patient whose father died 25 years ago. The patient still has not gotten over the death of his father. The guilt about the death of his father arises from the belief that he could have saved his father when he died at an early age. This patient feels a lack of entitlement, and he believes that he is not entitled to live any longer than his father did. His father was 50 at his death and when the patient turned 50 he experienced depression.

The patient's history shows self-sabotage and periods of depression and guilt. I want to help him appreciate that when he is recalling his father he is not recalling the happy times and the positive relationship he had, nor the memories of his father that have enriched his life. He is recalling, the majority of the time, the experience of what it was like when his father died. The patient is not recalling his father, he is recalling a painful event that he experienced that had intense emotional repercussions. The approach is to ask the patient to think back on the number of times that he has thought about his father and ask what percentage of those times he would estimate they were happy thoughts and what percentage they were thoughts about the death. Invariably the majority of the times will be thoughts of the death. It is important to interpret to the patient: "So you are not thinking of your father, you are thinking of the painful experience of his loss." It is an important distinction to tease out the difference between a memory of a significant person and the sadness that pervades that memory. The patient does not understand that he is relating to the memory of that experience and not to the person. The experience becomes for him the object relation and he confuses it with the memory of his father. Educating the patient and helping the patient understand that this is true goes a long way toward facilitating the patient's ability to view the relationship clearly. It is no different than in the termination, when we talk about the goodbye and what is in the goodbye, that it is appropriate that one is sad to say goodbye and it is appropriate to feel the sadness but to keep in mind, and this is interpreted to the patient, that "a part of me will go with you where ever you go, and a part of you will go with me where ever I go." All relationships have to come to an end. The ability to tolerate loss is the cornerstone of mental health. There is an expiration date on everything in the universe. Appreciating how enriching the relationship was and how that part of the relationship will always live within us is an important component of tolerating loss. The way to facilitate someone achieving that kind of healthy outlook is to interpret to them how much emphasis they place on a recalled event rather than the person, and how that event becomes the object relation. It is equally important that the person list the positives and negatives about a relationship.

Dean continues to discuss the loss of his father.

Zois: What did you lose when you lost your father?

Dean: I don't know. I don't know if I liked him or whether I didn't like him, whether I hated him or whether I loved him. I feel in some ways that I lost a good friend.

Zois: Can you tell me about that?

Dean: Well, there is this tremendous ambivalence there.

Zois: You say that you feel that you lost a good friend?

Go to the positive when it is offered. It saves time. I ignore the ambivalence because he has acknowledged it. I focus instead on the comment, "a good friend."

Dean: Yes.

Zois: What was that like?

Dean: We used to have a lot of fun together. We used to golf together and play bridge together. After he died I used to sit in his chair for bridge.

Zois: How do you feel as you think about that?

He recalls positive events. It is important to bring the emotion into the therapy room so that the patient can experience the feeling in the moment.

Dean: Sad.

Zois: In many ways you wanted to be close to this man?

Dean: Yes.

Zois: And there are many times you had happy, close experiences?

Dean: Yes. I wanted to screw my mother, too.

Zois: You want to give me the picture you are an unfeeling person as we are looking at the close feelings that you had with your father. You don't want me to see you as a tender feeling man. You don't want me to *penetrate into your life.*

This is a transference interpretation. The patient does not want me to see him as a tender, feeling man, in part due to guilt and lack of entitlement and in part due to the implications of homosexual fears. I purposefully choose the word "penetrate" in this instance to work with the homosexual issue.

Dean: Why do you say that? Maybe I really wanted that.

Zois: That's not where we are now, is it? That's another issue. You notice how you move away from those feelings? We were there, remembering how you filled in for him at the bridge game, carried on those feelings, tried to be with him in that way, you remember a very positive connection and you want to run away from it and me.

Dean: You don't think I really had—

Zois: That is not the issue we are discussing. You want to divert me with your guilt.

Dean: Because the feelings are so sad I don't want to deal with them.

Zois: Let's look at them. Here you are feeling sad and then you punish yourself with incest fantasies.

Dean: I don't understand how that becomes a form of punishment.

Zois: You said to me with recrimination in your voice "I want to screw my mother." What you're saying is, "I don't deserve to have these positive feelings with my father. Look at what else I've done." So you draw that wedge between you and people close to you and you take it out on yourself and take revenge on yourself.

Dean: The real feeling is that I hate me.

Zois: Feeling guilty for all of this?

Dean: Guilty of what?

Zois: You tell me. We know that you have intense guilt about your father's death.

Dean: Okay.

Zois: So intense that you haven't been able to say goodbye to him, that even when you look at the positive relationship, you go back to the guilt as if you don't deserve to be free. The sadness moves over to guilt.

Dean: The guilt is that I wanted him to die.

Zois: Did you have that thought?

Dean: I must.

Zois: Can you document it? Did you think of him as out of the picture?

Dean: The thought that I have is that I wanted him to die so that I could have my mother.

Zois: But if you can't document that, then we have a piece of evidence that can't be validated.

Dean: I can't document that.

Zois: What brings that thought to your mind? Did you worry about that?

Dean: His health? He was never sick.

Zois: Did you ever have any thoughts that he would die in a car accident or anything else?

Dean: Nothing that comes to mind.

Zois: So where does this guilt come from that you wanted him to die so that you could have your mother? Did you learn that in therapy?

Dean: No, it was just a thought that came to mind.

Zois: Where did it come from?

Dean: I don't know.

Zois: Did you read it somewhere?

Dean: It just comes to mind. That's all. So when it comes to mind, there must be some basis for it, or am I trying now to invent something to do the same thing all over again? I don't know.

Zois: You see you are telling me, aside from the time that he kicked you and you had a rage reaction here, what he did then which filled you with guilt, you are unable to document it.

Dean: Then that rage must have been so strong that I wanted to kill him or I wanted him to be dead then.

Zois: But can you recall, as you were there on the floor and he kicked you, the emotion that you had?

Dean: No.

Zois: Well, we can piece it together. We see that you can't talk about your father to this day without tears, without sadness, without guilt. So we know that you haven't resolved your relationship, that you never said goodbye to him.

In this segment I cover every issue he has brought up: guilt about his father, guilt about his mother, and lack of entitlement. However, I summarize the focus of our work in this session: the ability to come to terms with his relationship with his father. I interpret his incest fantasy as self-punishment, something he manufactured to beat himself up and to avoid resolving his relationship with his father.

MOVING TOWARD INTIMACY

Intimacy is a concept that is easily misconstrued. When people speak of intimacy they usually associate it with being physically intimate or in love with someone. For our purposes we apply a broader definition of the term. Intimacy encompasses the ability to allow a friend, relative, spouse, or loved one to share our deepest emotions, concerns, worst fears, and highest aspirations. One of the goals of therapy is to accomplish this kind of intimacy in the transference. That is the key to unlock the door that has been obstructing the individual from being intimate with others. We cannot make the assumption that the concept of intimacy is interpreted in the same way by everyone. Frequently you will have patients who have been intimate with someone and have lost that person, either through death or divorce or other reasons beyond their control. In those situations the concept of intimacy is connected to the painful experience of loss. The patient equates intimacy with painful emotions and guards against them in the transference. The patient understandably tries to defeat the therapist's attempts to be close. Here again this issue underscores the importance of the therapist applying challenge and focus on the defense to create the intimacy necessary to bring about change. Intimacy may also generate anxiety because of homoerotic impulses or fears.

This vignette illustrates the anxiety related to homoerotic fears. In this particular session I made a classic short-term therapy observation when Herbert was talking about his relationship with his father.

Zois: So you cheated your father of a son.

Herbert: I never looked at it that way. I always talked about his remoteness.

When a patient talks about the distance or the coldness of a parent it is important to examine how much the patient contributed to the distancing. That is the most therapeutic approach. The session ended shortly after the above exchange. When the patient returned the next week he seemed to be somewhat at loose ends, tending to look away, seeming subdued. He began the session by stating that what we had discussed last week had been very revelatory to him—the notion that he had pushed his father away. He thought about his relationship with his son and how he had rationalized why he was not as close to his son as he might want to be. He appears anxious so I move to the transference.

Zois: How do you feel with me right now?

Herbert: I feel a little uncomfortable.

Zois: What comes to your mind?

Herbert: It's almost like there is something sexual between the two of us. I don't know where that thought came from, it just popped into my mind.

Zois: What comes to your mind?

Herbert: I admire certain things about you and there have been times from time to time I have thought to myself, "Is this a sexual thing? Am I having homosexual thoughts about my therapist?"

Zois: So you want to be close to me?

Herbert: Yes.

Zois: What comes to your mind?

Herbert: As I said there are certain things that I admire. I want to be like you when I grow up.

Zois: You want to have the relationship with me that you didn't have with your father.

Herbert: Yes, I think about how it would be to be close not only to you but to my son.

Zois: You started this session today by talking about cheating your father of a relationship. Did you want to be close to your father as you look at it now?

Herbert: Yes.

Zois: You crave closeness. Being close to me or being close to your son would be a way of making up for that closeness that you denied yourself.

Herbert: I didn't think about that part of it but now that you say it.

I could see in the patient's face relief that the sexual material had a basis in non-sexual issues. Technically, I interpret homoerotic feelings that are based on tender feelings with the statement, "So you want to be close to me." When this interpretation is made the patient becomes much less anxious. I go on to make another interpretation about his relationship with his son and his relationship with me.

Zois: You tell me that there is a part of you that doesn't believe that you're entitled to have a relationship with your son or with me. For instance when your son asks you to go on vacation with him, you rationalize why you couldn't spare the time to go away. In therapy here there have been times when you've avoided me. There was that block of time when you told me that you didn't call to reschedule a session for several months because you said you couldn't afford it. But as we look at it now you were avoiding me. You knew you could work out a fee payment, didn't you?

Herbert: Yes.

Zois: So what are your thoughts now?

Herbert: I can see that I've had some anxiety about being close to you.

Now I point out something that is very important.

Zois: That anxiety is born of the thought that because you cheated your father of a son that you are not entitled to have a close relationship with any other man, whether it's your son or me or a friend. Didn't you once say to me that all of your friends are women?

Herbert: Yes [Smiling].

The interpretation of lack of entitlement should follow the interpretation of tender feelings and intimacy because the one issue dynamically gives rise to the other: cheating the father results in guilt, that is, the patient is not entitled to any closeness or happiness. Craving closeness with his father, which he did not experience, translates to homoerotic fantasies as a means of creating that closeness.

4

Overview of the Evaluation

The initial evaluation, which can take an hour or up to several hours, sets the tone of the relationship between therapist and patient. Here the therapist learns the strengths of the patient, how defensive the patient is, and how connected or disconnected to his or her emotions. The therapist explores with the patient the fundamental issues. Some of the most important of these issues are:

- The patient's ability to act on his or her own behalf vs. self-sabotage
- Dependence vs. independence
- Inappropriate attachment to another person vs. the ability to say goodbye
- Action vs. passivity
- The ability to tolerate loss vs. chronic grieving

- Emotional isolation vs. the ability to experience feelings
- Distancing vs. intimacy

DIAGNOSTIC AND THERAPEUTIC ASPECTS OF THE EVALUATION

The initial interview is both a diagnostic interview and an important therapeutic session. The patient must leave the session improved to at least some degree. The implications of no improvement is a poor prognosis for the therapy. An evaluation in which there has been no improvement is grounds for questioning whether the therapist has utilized the technique effectively. If that has been the case and there still has been no improvement, the patient may not be a candidate for STT.

Making the diagnosis during the evaluation is, of course, important. In terms of a diagnosis, the therapist is interested primarily in whether the patient can tolerate the impact of his or her unconscious material. Can the patient tolerate the emotions generated in the therapeutic process? The degree and kinds of defenses the patient utilizes are also assessed.

Most important, if the evaluation is to be considered effective, there has to be a penetration past the defenses to feelings and thoughts that have caused the patient pain. Those thoughts and feelings have to be brought to the patient's awareness, and that awareness should be associated with an emotional response. The lack of an emotional response has negative implications for the success of the therapy. Again, the patient must experience the impulse component of the defense in the transference.

THE THERAPIST'S GOAL IN THE EVALUATION

The initial interview must accomplish several things for the therapist. It must:

- Provide a clear picture of the areas of disturbance
- Allow the therapist to assess the patient's defenses, which the therapist challenges from the outset
- Allow the therapist to assess the size of the gap between the patient's thoughts and feelings
- Enable the therapist to relate the patient's current problems to past issues, so that the patient can experience in the transference emotions he or she has buried
- Provide opportunities for intimacy between therapist and patient during which the patient demonstrates emotion
- Generate enough information so that the therapist can develop a strategy
- Enable the therapist to estimate how many sessions the treatment will require.

OUTLINE OF THE EVALUATION

I. Assessing the Areas of Disturbance

The initial evaluation opens with a question: "Can you tell me what your problems are?" In response to your questions, the patient says "I'm depressed." Your next question is not "How long have you been depressed?" but "What do you mean when you say you're depressed?" Do not make the mistake of assuming that the patient's vocabulary is the same as the therapist's—it is not. When the patient says, "I'm depressed," the therapist must ask, "What do you mean when you say 'depressed'?" "Well, I feel sad." "What do you mean by 'sad'? Can you elaborate?" "I feel a sense of worthlessness, like I have nothing much in my life, I haven't accomplished anything, and so on." Then the next question is, "How do you experience that sense of worthlessness?"

II. Detailing the Patient's History

The examination of the areas of disturbance will provide some history as well as some information about the defenses the patient utilizes. Therefore, the length of time the first phase of the evaluation takes will vary. The following information should be elicited. Some of these questions will cause anxiety and therefore defensiveness. The rule that any exchange of information in the face of resistance is valueless continues to apply.

- Where were you born?
- Where did you live? House, apartment?
- Who lived with you?
- What were the sleeping arrangements? Who slept where?
- Where did you sleep in relation to your parent's room?
- What did your mother look like when you were growing up? Describe her figure. Did you ever see her naked?
- What did your father look like when you were growing up? Describe his appearance. Did you ever see him naked?

- How did your mother behave toward you?
- How did your father behave toward you?
- How did your parents behave towards each other?
- Did they demonstrate emotion in front of the children?
- Did you have evidence they were having sex? What was it?
- Who are you closer to?
- Do you have any brothers or sisters?
- Where are you in terms of the ages of your siblings?
- Which sibling were you closest to?
- Who was your mother closer to in your mind?
- Who was your father closer to in your mind?
- Who were you named for?

What's in a name? Sometimes the answer yields a great deal of useful information. On more than one occasion the response to "Who were you named for?" opened the door that led to core neurotic conflicts. Biff is a 34-year-old male who entered therapy because he was unable to commit to marry his fiancée of two years. She was threatening to call off the engagement if the matter was not resolved. He had been in therapy several years before for a similar issue with another girlfriend. His therapist, a colleague, had moved out of state. During the evaluation he was describing an incident at a party where he became enraged at his fiancée's boss for making fun of his name.

Zois: What did he say about your name?

Biff: The jerk was rhyming it like some kind of grammar school loser.

Zois: How did you feel?

Biff: I felt like ripping his head off. I tore into him. My fiancée was embarrassed.

Zois: Had this ever happened before?

Biff: Are you kidding? I've had to put up with crap about my name all of my life.

Zois: Who are you named for?

Biff: I don't know, some jerk my mother was dating before she married my father.

Bingo. In treatment the patient was able to come to terms with his anger at his mother and the mistrust he harbored toward women in general. He married, and on three-year follow-up reported he no longer experienced angry outbursts at the slightest provocation. His relationship with his wife was a source of happiness for him. His therapy had taken ten hours.

Mary Ann was a 27-year-old who came to treatment for depression. She was unable to sustain relationships and was inappropriately attached to her parents, whom she described as "running her life." She described herself as "unhappy" and "worthless." During the evaluation she talked about a sister who died before the patient was born. Her parents named her for her dead sister.

Mary Ann: Mary Ann! Mary Ann! [sobbing] It's always about her. They [her parents] don't care about me. All they talk about is Mary Ann. They wish she was here and not me. I went to her grave last month.

Zois: How did you feel when you were at the cemetery?

Mary Ann: Angry. I can't be a 9-year-old dead girl. I want my own life. They won't let me have it.

Zois: In your mind, you're a hostage to your parents. You say they won't let you have your life. But you are the only one who can take charge of your life.

Mary Ann: They won't let me.

Zois: So you want to go through life a victim.

The patient was able to clarify her anger at her parents for attempting to resolve their grief and guilt through her. The bizarre action of naming her for her deceased sister was a dramatic example of the distorted relationship they had with the patient. It was her reaction to her name at the outset of therapy that pointed the way to her lifelong anger and guilt that translated to the depression she suffered. Mary Ann's treatment took thirty eight sessions in contrast to Biff's ten, due to the greater number of deep-seated issues that had to be resolved.

Less dramatic illustrations of naming involve a patient who was named for his maternal grandfather. His mother idolized her deceased father and projected these impulses onto her son. One of the issues in his treatment was the belief that he was the living representation of a dead man.

The patient's sex life and the recurrent themes in his or her masturbatory fantasies are important because frequently they yield information as to the core neurotic issues.

- How frequently do you have sex?
- What kind of sex do you prefer? What are your favorite positions and favorite forms of sex—vaginal, anal, oral, etc.?

- When did you first masturbate?
- When did you first have intercourse?
- What are your fantasies when you masturbate?
- What are your fantasies when you have intercourse? Is there a recurring fantasy?
- Is there more than one person in your fantasy?

Anger must first be gauged in terms of intensity. Then it must be desensitized so that the patient can view the anger without experiencing anxiety and discomfort. The process of desensitization is achieved by having the patient elaborate in detail the circumstances and experience of the anger.

- How angry were you?
- What did you see in your mind?
- Did you have the thought of lashing out?
- What would he or she look like if you did that?
- How do you feel right now as you think of that?

This line of questioning enables the patient to tolerate the emotions generated by anger. The same questions have to be asked when dealing with anger in the transference.

The death of a significant person is dealt with in the same manner.

- When was the last time you saw him or her alive?
- What did he look like?
- What did you say to him?
- How did you find out he had died?
- How did he look when you saw him dead?
- What was the funeral like?
- Where is he buried?
- When is the last time you went to the cemetery?

- How do you feel as you think of this?
- So you never said goodbye to him.
- If he were here today, what would you want to say to him?

The above questions provide a basis for understanding the issues that contribute to the patient's psychodynamic makeup. Obviously they are not intended to be read to the patient as a script. Challenging resistance and defenses will lead to elaboration and other avenues of information. However, viewed as building blocks these questions will help the therapist stay focused.

5

The Evaluation

There are a few issues to keep in mind in terms of evaluations in general. The goal of the evaluation is to determine what the patient's problems are, what you are going to do about those problems, and how many sessions will be required. The evaluation should not constitute a one-way street where you gain information and the patient gains nothing except providing a history. At the end of the evaluation the patient must leave with an increased awareness of the conflicts that have caused his or her unhappiness. You have to have at least opened the door a little bit so that the patient can look into the future and see, perhaps for the first time, a life free of the burdens he or she has been carrying. There are a couple of rules to follow. The first is to exercise the rule of abstinence. The therapist should not divulge personal information in response to the patient, so that the transference is not distorted by the therapist's characteristics. When you first meet the patient you introduce yourself and then you usher the patient to the therapy chair. If the patient is chatting with you on the way you do not respond. Do not say anything that will reveal personal facts or opinions you may hold in general. If the patient says "It's a beautiful day out," you simply nod, do not engage in chit-chat from the outset. The other rule is that the patient is informed of the videotaping before the patient comes to the office. That should be done with the patient on the phone and a release should be signed by the patient in the waiting room. If the patient has questions about the release then obviously you answer them directly. The therapy is conducted seated, facing one another, optimally in chairs that are similar if not identical to one another. The majority of patients will come in, whether they have been in therapy before or not, with an overdetermined and overvalued view of the therapist. That viewpoint feeds into the patient's tendency to be passive and allow the "expert" to do the work. The therapist will not avoid the work by general discussions about issues that are not relevant. By the end of the evaluation the therapist should be prepared to summarize the issues that have confronted the patient and make an educated guess, based on what has been discovered, as to how long the therapy will take. That estimate becomes easier with time as more and more patients are treated. In time you will readily gauge within the first hour (if not sooner) from the history, the degree of resistance, and the types of defenses how long the case will take.

AREAS OF DISTURBANCE

Dean is a 53-year-old male who comes to therapy because he experiences rage, physical pain, and unhappiness in relationships. He is divorced and has a son and a daughter. He is in a partnership in a successful business.

Zois: Can you tell me what your problems are?

Dean: I'm in trouble and I'm aware of it.

Zois: What do you mean?

Dean: I am physically in trouble. I'm very uncomfortable from a number of problems that I suspect have a certain psychosomatic background. I think for once in my life I would like to get my head straightened out.

Zois: What are those problems?

Dean: Well, the most recent interesting one was of an unknown origin when I went into cardiopulmonary arrest for absolutely no reason whatsoever. Now, there are many cardiologists and neurologists that say there has got to be a reason for it even if we can't find it. I've come to the conclusion that may be the reason for it. It had nothing to do with the actual results.

Zois: What causes you to say that?

Dean: Just my own feeling about it, that's all.

Zois: How do you feel right now as you are thinking about it?

Technically, when the patient is giving us a description of a feeling, we want to bring that feeling into the room and have him experience it in the moment.

Dean: Anxious.

I do not accept the concept "anxious" because I do not know what he means by "anxious." Never assume that the vocabulary of the patient and the therapist are the same—always ask for elaboration.

He explains that his anxiety is reflected to him in terms of muscle spasm, pain in various parts of his body, and he feels warm.

Zois: What are you experiencing right now?

Dean: I'm probably running a temperature, which is not unusual for me to do at will at any time. I'm very warm. I'm in a tremendous amount of neck, shoulder, and rectal pain, I mean, right this minute.

I then want to know at what other times this happens.

Zois: Under what other circumstances do you feel this way?

Dean: It happens frequently enough and there is medical support for some disc problems in my neck, but I notice that when things are bothering me on some kind of emotional basis, the pain is far greater.

ELABORATION

Zois: Can you give me an illustration of that?

I always try to be specific, and I always seek elaboration.

Dean: Of the kind of thing emotionally that can trigger it?

Zois: Yes.

Dean: Not really off the top of my head. When they happen—I'm a good one for blocking things out, I guess.

Zois: You say "you guess" that you are blocking?

A challenge to the general defense of "I guess."

Dean: I'm sure I am blocking.

Zois: You smile when you say that.

Dean: Because I realize what the words "I guess" mean.

The patient puts me on notice that he is able to observe these defenses immediately. The educative process, I know right now, in terms of the defenses, will not be that difficult.

I now move to the transference. He has related to me that he is anxious, and that always has transferential implications. Who is he relating to? He is relating to the therapist; he is talking to me. He is not anxious in a vacuum; that cannot be ignored. Therefore, at this point I am comfortable to ask him how he is feeling in the transference.

Zois: So how are you feeling now as I'm asking you these questions?

Dean: I'm uptight.

Zois: Are you vague like this with other people?

Dean: Yes.

Zois: What comes to your mind?

Dean: It's a good way of avoiding the issue.

Zois: Who are you this way with besides me?

Dean: Anytime I want to avoid something.

Zois: Can you be specific?

Dean: My partners, and a particular gal that I see quite a bit of.

Zois: Can you tell me about her?

Dean: What can I tell you about her?

Zois: Can you tell me about her?

Dean: Oh, sure. I could talk to you about her for hours and the fact that you asked the question, it's almost as if there is a blank, a blank space. I'm quite annoyed at her right now, so maybe that's the reason.

Zois: What are you annoyed about?

Dean: Some attitudinal things that have happened within the last week or so.

Zois: That really doesn't tell me anything.

I challenge the vagueness.

Dean: I didn't like her comment that she made yesterday about my children. I didn't like her behavior for a number of days last week concerning her birthday, of how it was to be celebrated or her present that I bought her.

Zois: How does that make you feel?

Dean: Sometimes fantastic and sometimes very uncomfortable.

Zois: You say, annoyed?

Dean: Yes.

Zois: How annoyed are you?

Technically when a patient says he is angry, you want to find out how that anger expresses itself and the degree of that anger.

Dean: Annoyed enough that I walked out last night to give her a rest for some period of time.

Zois: That's not a description of your annoyance. It's a description of how you deal with your anger. You deal with it by avoidance. You walked out. How annoyed were you at that minute?

I make the interpretation on how he deals with anger defensively by avoidance.

Dean: Quite.

Zois: You were very annoyed?

Dean: Yes.

Zois: You were angry with her?

Dean: Oh, I'm probably one of the world's angry young men. I remember being angry.

Zois: Did you give her any information that you were angry?

Dean: Absolutely.

Zois: How did you do that?

Dean: Just by the conversation.

Zois: How did you tell her that you were angry?

Dean: She said to me, "Will you call me when you get home?" And I said, "I don't think so." She said, "Will you call me in the morning?" And I said, "I doubt it."

Zois: So you communicated your anger in a secondary way?

Dean: Yeah.

Zois: By implication?

Dean: Yes. I said some things that obviously I was angry when I said them.

Zois: What was that?

Dean: I said, "You know, unless you do something about this problem of selective memory. . . . "

Zois: So you were being reasonable?

Dean: Yes.

Zois: Talking about her problem with selective memory and by implication you told her you were angry because you weren't going to call her that night when you got home or the next morning, but in fact you didn't get angry with her directly. The way you were feeling inside wasn't the way that you were coming across.

Dean: I have a bad problem with anger in terms of temperament.

Zois: So the question was—

Dean: I try to control it.

Zois: You were controlling yourself then?

Dean: Absolutely.

Zois: What?

Dean: Yes.

Zois: Now, you say you have a problem with your temper?

Dean: Yes.

At this point, it is important to assess how much of a problem he has with his temper, and how much impulse control he has. You want to determine if this is a patient who has the ability to lash out at you physically. That determination is best ascertained by the past history. The other important factor is your sense of the individual in the room. This patient does report striking out at his girlfriend but my experience with him in the room is that he is not a threat to me physically. As I ask questions my belief is reinforced.

Zois: What happens to it?

Dean: Anything could happen.

Zois: Give me an illustration.

Dean: Physically I can hurt people.

Zois: Who would you hurt physically?

Dean: Anyone—many people.

Zois: Still, that doesn't tell me anything.

Dean: Whoever gets in my way when I'm in that kind of mood.

Zois: You are not giving me an illustration. You are not telling me.

Dean: I've hurt Kim.

Zois: What happened? What did you do?

Dean: I kicked her around a few times.

Zois: What caused you to get so angry at her that you lashed out?

I am now aware that his impulse control is very low as I am assessing his potential for anger.

Dean: Unfortunately, that's one of the problems that I'm aware of. I can't tell you. It must be some build-up and then some small thing can just trigger it and it just flies.

Zois: So you are not in touch with your feeling then. Is that it?

Dean: I'm not sure.

Zois: So last night, did you want to lash out at her?

Dean: Probably.

Zois: You say "probably." Is it yes or is it no?

Dean: I don't know.

Zois: So what evidence do you have that you didn't?

Dean: She didn't want me to leave and I just wanted to get the hell out of there. So I left.

Zois: What were the angry thoughts toward Kim?

Dean: What do I need her for? What do I want to be around her for?

Zois: That's a description.

Dean: I was very angry. And I've said the statement about rectal pain and pain in the ass. I think she's the pain in my ass right now.

Zois: Last night when you were home and you were angry, were you having any pains?

Dean: Yes.

Zois: Where were the pains?

Dean: I just said, rectal pain and tremendous pain in my shoulder.

Zois: And pain in your shoulder?

Dean: And I think to some degree I worked that out. It's usually in my left shoulder and I'm left-handed. I suspect it has something to do with the wish of destroying someone, beating them or killing them or whatever.

Zois: Did you have the thought of killing her?

Dean: Conscious thought, absolutely not.

Zois: You have the thought now that it has to do with killing somebody.

Dean: Yes.

Zois: Who do you want to kill?

Dean: The world.

Zois: That's too general again.

Dean: Anyone who stands in my way.

Zois: Again, that's a general statement.

Dean: That's an honest statement.

He moves from vagueness to intellectualization.

Zois: But it doesn't help us understand. See, the question is: Who do you want to kill?

Dean: Would you like to stay here the rest of the afternoon? I think that's how long my list is.

Zois: You are anxious when I ask you that question?

Dean: I became anxious because the first thought that came to my mind was first my mother and then my brother.

Zois: That made you uncomfortable?

Dean: I was going to answer, "I suspect it did," but the answer is: yes, obviously it did.

Zois: Why do you want to kill your mom?

Dean: She laid a little guilt trip yesterday on me which annoyed me, so that obviously bothered me.

Zois: You want to kill her for one guilt trip?

Dean: Oh, no. she's been doing it all my life, so 50 years of it that I probably want to kill her for.

Zois: Again, you say "probably." So all your life you see her as doing what to you?

Dean: Well, I can't answer that question in terms of all of my life. I was 26 years old when my father died, and ever since then it's been just one continuous guilt trip. It bothers me.

Zois: How many people are in your family?

Dean: Just my brother and myself, and two parents.

Zois: How old is your brother?

Dean: My brother will be 55 in two weeks.

Zois: How old are you?

Dean: Fifty-three.

Zois: And your mother, how old is she?

Dean: Eighty-two.

Zois: And your dad, how old was he when he died?

Dean: Fifty-four.

Zois: What did he die from?

Dean: Cancer.

Zois: Of what?

Dean: Stomach.

Zois: Where were you raised?

Dean: In New York.

Zois: Where in New York?

Dean: New York City.

Zois: Your dad, what did he do?

Dean: He was an accountant.

Zois: And your mother?

Dean: A schoolteacher.

In an attempt to keep his level of anxiety tolerable, when he talks about homicidal fantasies, I ask him for more historical information. He has no cognitive disassociation—no trouble focusing or thinking—so he is integrated. The concepts that he is talking about are somewhat on an intellectual level, but I am keeping in mind his history. Even though he is integrated and they are fantasies, he does lash out.

The one thing I did not do, which is important, is I did not assess to what degree he injured his girlfriend. Did he push her, or did it require a visit to the emergency room? That is important information to gain because you need to be aware of the level of impulse control when you are challenging the defenses and evoking anxiety and anger in a patient who has a history of lashing out. However, my experience of him in the room relating to me is that he has an observing ego and is in control of his emotions.

Zois: What was it like growing up in that household with the two of them?

Dean: I didn't like it.

RESISTANCE

Zois: What didn't you like about it?

Dean: Here we go again. I don't know.

Now he is getting anxious and resistant, so I move to the transference. I reflect on his body, and keep challenging the vagueness.

Zois: How do you feel right now?

Dean: I can think of places that I would much rather be.

Zois: Your foot is moving and you're anxious now. Right?

Dean: Yes.

Zois: What was your relationship like with your mother when you were growing up before your father died?

Dean: No recollection.

Zois: Same with your father?

Dean: I loved my father.

Zois: Which one did you get along with better?

Dean: Probably my mother.

Zois: You say "probably"?

Dean: My mother.

Zois: Which one would be the one you would confide in?

Dean: My immediate reaction is to say neither.

Zois: But of the two?

Dean: My mother. I was going to put in a "probably" but we would have repeated that.

Zois: And your brother?

Dean: My brother was a pain in the ass since he was born. He's quite ill.

Zois: What's wrong with him?

Dean: Well, for the last ten years, he's had an

inoperable brain tumor, but prior to that he was just a pain in the ass.

Zois: What was he like growing up in the household?

Dean: Totally different than I was; brilliant, totally nonathletic. We were not close in any way at all.

Zois: Who did he get along with better, your mother or your father?

Dean: I don't think he had any relationship with my father at all.

Zois: And your mother?

Dean: Pretty good one.

Zois: Who did your mother favor between you and your brother?

Dean: My brother.

Zois: You smiled as you said that.

Dean: Because my brother had no relationship whatsoever with my father.

Zois: But you smiled as you said that she favored your brother.

Dean: I suspect every sibling probably thinks that.

Zois: Let's forget about every sibling for now. How do you feel right now as you are thinking about it?

Dean: I was sitting here thinking I don't even remember what you asked me. What was the question?

Zois: So it's very upsetting to you.

Dean: Well, the anxiety it brings on.

Zois: So that shows that there was an intense relationship with your mother.

Dean: Between my brother and my mother.

Zois: Between you and your mother.

Dean: Sure.

Zois: And you have an emotional reaction at the thought that she favored your brother.

Dean: Okay.

Zois: You smiled, but you don't want to tell me those feelings?

Dean: I don't know what they are.

Zois: See, you become vague now.

I challenge the defenses.

Dean: Well, you can say "vague" and I can't deny that it's not true.

I observe that he is getting agitated, so I say to him:

Zois: So are you irritated with me when I'm asking you these questions?

Dean: Trying not to be.

Zois: But you are having the impulse?

Dean: Oh, sure.

Next I make an interpretation and examine the transference. I point out to him that his level of irritation and anxiety has increased when I touch on the subject of his mother.

Zois: So on the one hand you come here to find some relief for these problems, and on the other hand when I talk about this relationship between you and your mother you become irritated?

Dean: I must in some way.

Zois: Now you are intellectualizing.

Dean: Okay.

PRIOR TREATMENT

Zois: Have you ever been in therapy before?

Dean: Absolutely.

Zois: Can you tell me about that?

Dean: Sure. I spent two years with Fred Borden. I was seeing him anywhere from twice a week to five times a week. So it was an absolute waste.

Zois: When was that?

Dean: '76, '77, '78, somewhere in there.

Zois: Were you vague with him?

Dean: This was true Freudian analysis on the couch. I don't know that you can answer it in terms of being vague. He never said a word, so what was there to be vague about?

Zois: What did you get out of that therapy?

Dean: Nothing at all.

When the patient is negative about the former therapist, it is tempting not to say anything and in that way covertly agree that the other therapist must have been far inferior to the present therapist. Therapeutically there is no mileage to be gained from that. The best thing to do technically is to use what you know about the patient to make an interpretation as to how the patient defeated the other therapist. You will gain more in terms of bringing about change in the patient. Having the patient examine self-sabotaging behavior and impulses, rather than overtly or covertly agreeing with the patient's point of view in terms of prior therapies is the most productive approach.

Zois: Yet you continued to go for two years?

Dean: Yes.

Zois: What's the reason you give yourself?

Dean: I thought that at some point there would be a breakthrough or something would happen.

Zois: How did you terminate?

Dean: I said goodbye.

Zois: How did you do that?

This to my mind is one of the most important questions that can be asked. It will give you valuable information. I would always ask residents in supervision, "If you had one question to ask a patient about their prior therapy, what would it be?" I always instructed them to ask, "How did you say goodbye?" From that goodbye you will learn much about how the patient has dealt with significant people in his or her life. You will be able to assess the patient's ability to tolerate loss, which speaks volumes in any therapy.

Dean: I tried to explain to him that I felt that I was getting absolutely nothing out of it, that it was time to leave.

Zois: You say you tried to. Did you succeed?

Dean: I have no idea.

Zois: Were you—

Dean: His statement when I left was, "There is a lot of leaving going on in your life." He was referring to the fact that I was leaving my wife and my son. My daughter had just left to go to college and I was leaving her.

ANGER/HURT

Zois: How did you feel about that comment that he made?

Dean: I don't think I felt anything.

Zois: You remember the comment, but you don't remember having any feelings about it?

Dean: No.

Zois: How do you feel about him now?

Dean: No feelings about him whatsoever.

Zois: You spent two years, two to five times a week?

Dean: There was a bad mix there, that's all.

Zois: There was a bad mix, but you have no feelings toward him at all?

Dean: No. I don't like him. I don't dislike him. Your question does not in any way invoke a great amount of anger.

Zois: The word anger comes to your mind.

Technically, when patients deny a thought or emotion, use the same word they use to turn it around on them: "The word anger comes to your mind."

Dean: Yes, but I can't relate to it.

I elect to drop this line of questioning in order to avoid an impasse. I elicit more history about any other prior therapies. I will have ample opportunity to return to the issue of anger.

Zois: Have you had any other therapy?

Dean: There were some recent ones I've tried.

Zois: When was that?

Dean: Within the last few months. I saw somebody once who recommended that I see someone else and he gave me a list of names and I never did anything about it for a couple of months. Then I conveniently lost them and I called this guy again and he gave me another list of names. The first one was Jacobs. I saw him twice and we made an appointment for the third visit and after the second visit he called me in my office the next morning and he really took me by surprise. He said, "I don't think that we should see each other anymore." He said, "I don't want to end up another one of the Freudian assholes that you have described." And that was a direct quotation by him.

Zois: How did you feel about that?

Dean: I was quite surprised.

Zois: What was the emotional reaction?

Dean: I suspect rejection, probably.

Zois: You felt rejected, yes or no?

Dean: I just said it.

Zois: There is the "probably."

Dean: I just put those in. I thought it was in poor taste professionally to do it that way, but that's not my judgment to make.

Zois: You rationalize why you shouldn't have feelings about it.

Dean: Well, once somebody says that to you, my gut tells me, all right, I'm not professional enough in any way to be sure, but my own reaction was that his having said it, was to make the relationship impossible to work, so it really didn't matter what my feelings were in terms of his—

Zois: They mattered to you.

Dean: Of course they mattered to me.

Zois: *You want to minimize it.* In the two sessions you had with him, what was discussed?

Always point out when the patient minimizes emotions since this has implications as to how the patient handles emotions in general.

Dean: Anger, rage. I was very, very angry in that period.

Zois: Were you vague with him?

Dean: Sometimes. There were things that I was not vague about and there were other things that I was vague about.

Most of his defenses to this point have been of vagueness and generalization.

Zois: So what was it that led him to say that he didn't want to be one of the Freudian assholes that you described?

Dean: What did I think it was?

Zois: What did you say to him?

Dean: I asked him that question specifically.

Zois: What was the question that you asked?

Dean: What was it that made him come to this conclusion, that when I had left six o'clock the evening before we made an appointment for three days later? What had transpired? And his answer was that he had done a great deal of soul searching and that he did not feel that he was competent to treat me. What did I say to him that must have led him to that conclusion?

Zois: What did you say in terms of Freudian assholes?

Dean: I'm trying to remember the context of the statement.

Zois: You told him about other therapists?

Dean: Yeah. Somehow in the course of talking he made the statement that based upon things that I have said, that he was in a no-win position.

Zois: So basically he told you that *you had defeated him?*

Dean: There's no question about that. I had said to him in that second visit, I said to him, "You know, I suspect that you are afraid of me." And I think he was.

Again I interpret his self-sabotage. The patient reveals something very important that has transferential implications. He tells me how he defeated the prior therapist. By telling me that he believed that the former therapist was afraid of him, and going so far as to report that he verbalized this thought to the previous doctor, he is putting me on notice that he is going to attempt to intimidate me as a means of sabotaging the therapy. This had worked for him in the past.

Zois: What did you base that on?

Dean: It's a whole series of things. Something about coming up in the elevator.

Zois: Now you told me that you thought that he was afraid of you. Were you irritated with him?

Dean: No, I was not. I was very enraged, but I don't believe that it was at him.

Zois: Who else did you see after this doctor?

Dean: Jacobs?

Zois: Yes.

Dean: You.

Zois: That was it?

Dean: I saw someone before that who had recommended Jacobs.

Zois: What reason did the doctor have for—

Dean: He didn't have any time.

Zois: How did you feel about that?

Dean: I was quite annoyed by that.

Zois: How annoyed were you?

Dean: Very.

Zois: What did you see in your mind?

Dean: I don't know that I saw anything at that time. Now, my reaction is I didn't see anyone for a period of months. I liked this guy that I saw first, the guy whose name I can't remember, and I decided that I would see if his schedule freed up any. I called him back after the summer and it hadn't changed.

Zois: You asked him if he had time at that point?

Dean: Yes.

Zois: Was that the time you lost this list April or May to September?

Dean: Yes.

Zois: When you called back in September was it because you lost the list and wanted more names or was it because you wanted to see if he could take you in treatment?

Dean: I wanted to see, number one, if he could take me into treatment and number two, if he couldn't, I was beginning to feel, for the first time in my life, that I really wanted to do something.

Zois: So when you told me about it before you mentioned losing a list, but not that you had wanted to see if he had more time. So it was difficult for you to say that you wanted to see this man?

Dean: It might have been. That was not a conscious thought. But as you started to ask specific questions, it came back.

Zois: The first thing that came to mind was that you lost the list?

Dean: Yes.

Zois: But as you look at it you really called to see if he had more time?

Dean: Yes.

Zois: So how do you feel toward him? You said you were angry. What else were you feeling?

Dean: I don't know. Possibly rejected. Could be.

Zois: You say "possibly." Can you document it?

Dean: No.

Zois: With the second doctor did you talk about the man who referred you?

Dean: Yes.

Zois: What do you recall you talked about?

Dean: Only that I had seen him, that he had no time and that I waited a period of months. He still had no time and then I went about the rest of the list. I had it in my pocket.

Zois: So you were very angry when you had gotten to this second doctor?

Dean: Yes.

Zois: Angry at being turned away from the first doctor?

Dean: Not on a conscious level.

Zois: As we look at it?

Dean's comment, "Not on a conscious level," is a defense. He is resistant to acknowledge his feelings of hurt at being rejected by the therapist because this recapitulates the pain in his relationship with his father. His comment is an attempt to deflect me. The way around this is not to enter into a dialogue about whether it is conscious or unconscious, but to bring it into the transference: "As we look at it now, what do you think? As we're examining it together. As you look at it now, how do you feel as you think about that anger?"

It is important, when an individual is talking about a recalled event, and there is an emotion connected to that event, to examine how the individual experiences the feeling in the room. This is more important therapeutically than a description of what happened in the past. You always want them to bring the emotion into the room and experience it in the transference.

TRANSFERENCE

Always use the transference generously. Accomplishing intimacy in the transference is one of the major factors in a successful therapy. Also it will abort the development of a neurotic transference and it will facilitate terminating appropriately with the patient. You are treating the patient for a relatively brief period of time, so unless you focus on the transference, you are going to have difficulty accomplishing termination. You want to use the transference every time you have the opportunity.

SELF-SABOTAGE

Zois: You were angry, and you defeated him and you defeated yourself?

Dean: Yes, because in the conversation with Jacobs, he called me and told me that he didn't think it could work. It was on Friday morning and I happen to remember that he said to me that he would get in touch with whatever this guy's name was over the weekend and that I should call him on Monday and ask him what to do. And I did call him Monday. As I remember I didn't get him until Tuesday or something. We briefly talked about Jacobs' behavior and I made some comment to him that I thought that the guy was just not strong enough and his answer to that was that he had no way of evaluating that. I asked him what Jacobs had said to him and he chose not to discuss it.

Zois: How were you feeling as you were talking to him on the phone?

Dean: I don't recall. My gut tells me that I was probably angry as hell, but I honestly don't recall.

Zois: Have you ever thought that he might take you into treatment?

Dean: No. No, I did not.

Zois: So when I said to you that you had defeated him and defeated yourself you made the association with calling this first doctor.

Dean: I'm not sure that that's what happened in the mental process. I suspect that when you asked the question, it just triggered something.

Zois: How do you feel when I made that statement to you that you had defeated yourself by defeating the doctor?

I reiterate for him.

Dean: I didn't like the second part when you said "defeated yourself." I'm in total agreement with you that I defeated him.

Zois: But in the end who loses?

Dean: Well, we lose different kinds of things.

Zois: That's vague.

Dean: I don't think so.

Zois: Who is the one that is unhappy?

Dean: Well, I'm unhappy for my personal concerns. I suspect that he's got to be unhappy because he couldn't do something. I couldn't care less about his unhappiness.

Zois: You say his unhappiness is irrelevant. Who is the one who didn't get treatment?

Dean: I didn't.

Zois: So who is the one that's not feeling good?

Dean: Okay, on that basis it's me.

I make a summation of his self-sabotaging.

Zois: What other basis is there? You are smiling. We see as you come here, there is a part of you that wants to defeat yourself, take revenge. You tell me that you are unhappy. You tell me that you have a lot of problems; some of them are physical, others are psychological. Yet as I ask you questions there is a part of you that avoids and becomes vague and when I try to get into the relationship with your mother, you report the feeling of irritation.

Dean: All right. That's all true, but I think there has to be some validity to the fact that whatever these things are, they have not totally made an invalid out of me.

Here I explain to him that when he phrases it as denial—"they have not made an invalid out of me"—and this is important technically—he has the thought he is being made an invalid. I go on with that and stay with the self-defeat. He is having trouble acknowledging self-sabotage.

Zois: Now you become defensive.

Dean: No, I'm making a statement of fact.

Zois: No, you're telling me, "I'm not as bad off as you thought I was."

Dean: I don't know what you think.

Zois: You thought I thought you were an invalid. You say, "I'm not an invalid."

Dean: That whatever it is, it's not—

Zois: You're drawing conclusions. Is that getting me off the point about defeating yourself? You want to engage me now in a discussion about how incapacitated or not incapacitated you are. That's not the point. The point is: whatever the problems are, you have in the past tended to defeat yourself.

Dean: "In therapy," did you add? Was that the last two words?

Zois: Have you done it in other areas?

Dean: I'm not sure. Please, answer my question. "In therapy," was that what you said?

Zois: You want to tag on "in therapy" because you don't like the idea you defeat yourself.

Dean: Well, I run a pretty successful business.

Zois: My question was: Have you done it in other areas?

Dean: I'm sure I have.

Zois: "I'm sure I have" doesn't tell me anything. The question is: Have you ever defeated yourself in other areas? You come back with a general answer which is useless to me.

Dean: Yes, I have.

Zois: Can you give me an illustration?

Dean: I have forced personal relationships not to work, with my former wife, with other women. I have damn near destroyed a business and then built it back up again.

Zois: So this has occurred in other areas of your life?

Dean: Yes.

In the above exchange I say "You have defeated yourself," and this statement strikes a chord in him. He wants to avoid the concept by limiting it: "You mean in therapy." I say, "Have you done it in other areas?" He uses the defense of generalization and says, "I'm not sure." I focus on that and say, "You want to tag on 'in therapy' because you don't like the idea that you defeat yourself." Now he says he runs a successful business. He is still being defensive. I ask him again and he now goes from being "not sure" to "I'm sure I have." That is still vague, however, because he does not elaborate. I pick up on the vagueness in the next sentence. He becomes more specific and talks about personal relationships with his ex-wife and other women, and that he actually almost destroyed a business. This is another illustration that you cannot let even the most casual defense go by. When you focus on the defense the patient becomes clear in his mind that he has been self-defeating in other areas, whereas just a minute ago he was defensive about it and he was telling himself and me that he is not sure.

Zois: And it has occurred in your therapy to date?

Dean: Absolutely.

OEDIPAL TRIANGLES

Zois: Now, as I asked you about your mother favoring your brother, you pointedly become irritated at me that I had gotten into that subject.

Dean: Yes.

Zois: At this point what is your relationship like with your brother?

Dean: In his mind I am the greatest thing in this world.

Zois: And in your mind?

Dean: He is very infantile in some ways. He is extremely dependent, and yet he's got a heart of gold and is a good human being.

Zois: You say he was always a pain in the ass?

Dean: We never got along. We were never friends. We were never close.

Zois: But you say he feels close to you?

Dean: He adores me.

Zois: So to be accurate, he feels close to you?

Dean: Absolutely.

Zois: You don't feel close to him?

Dean: Totally correct.

Zois: That's the way it is?

Dean: Yes.

Zois: Was it that way right along?

Dean: Yes.

Zois: His relationship with your mother, in your mind what is that like?

Dean: He's extremely dependent upon her for all kinds of things.

Zois: What kinds of things?

Dean: If he wants to go somewhere, he's dependent upon her to take him. She still drives. If he needs something, he's dependent upon her to get it for him. He lives very close to her. He's dependent on her emotionally and socially.

Zois: He lives alone?

Dean: Yes.

Zois: How do you feel now as you are describing the relationship that he has with your mother?

Dean: Better him than me.

Zois: Was he dependent on your mother growing up?

Dean: Yes.

Zois: And you say she favored him?

Dean: That's what I perceive, yes.

Zois: What is it that made you feel that way?

Dean: It was obvious to me that my father had absolutely no use for him and I felt I was my father's favorite.

Zois: But what did you see in terms of your mother's favorite, and what evidence did you have that she favored him?

Dean: My recollection is that he always needed something and she would do it, where I was pretty much independent, both in getting into trouble and getting out of it.

Zois: On the one hand you say you didn't need her to do things for you, on the other hand you say she favored him. Is there a difference?

Dean: There is obviously a difference, but I think it was both.

Zois: But as far as she favored him, what did she do for him that she didn't do for you?

Dean: I don't know.

Zois: You have the feeling that she favored him?

Dean: Yes.

Zois: What's your reaction to that?

Dean: Jealousy.

Zois: So how does that jealousy make you feel?

Dean: Today or then or both?

The patient is now at the point where he can discuss his negative feelings towards his brother: he was jealous. When I ask him to connect the jealousy with an emotion he correctly asks, "Today or then or both?" As I have pointed out before, you want the patient to describe the emotion that he is experiencing with you in the room. That is the impulse component of the defense in the transference. He becomes defensive by saying nothing. I focus on that and I point out to him that he is compartmentalizing, because a little while ago he stated he would like to kill both of them.

Zois: Right now as you are thinking about it.

Dean: Nothing.

Zois: You say "nothing"?

Dean: Yes.

Zois: But a little while ago you said you would like to kill both of them.

Dean: To give you an example, I spoke to her on New Year's Day and she starts the conversation and I can tell by her voice that she's depressed and she's lonely and so on. She said, "You didn't call me last night at midnight." And I said, "Oh, I forgot." She said, "Do you realize since your father died that you never forgot to call me?" I was totally aware of it. I didn't feel like calling her.

Zois: So you are angry at her?

Dean: No. I didn't need that bullshit. I knew I didn't call her. She knew I didn't call her.

Zois: You are angry at her?

Dean: Yeah. That's typical of her little guilt games.

Zois: But you were angry the night before when you didn't call her.

Dean: No, I wasn't angry.

Zois: You weren't angry when you didn't call her? You say, "I don't need that bullshit."

Dean: I was aware of the fact that I didn't call her.

Zois: And didn't want to?

Dean: And didn't want to.

Zois: So you were angry at her?

Dean: No—yes, I was. I was because she had started with me the day before. She knew that both of my children were going to be with me all day Saturday and Sunday and she was looking for an invitation to join us. I didn't want her to. So what I must have done was say "Don't call her."

Zois: Say to who?

Dean: To myself.

Zois: So you were angry with her?

Dean: If you want to classify that as anger.

Zois: Let's be in agreement here. Is it anger or not?

Dean: It's annoyance. It's her typical pattern of guilt trips.

Zois: You want to minimize it here with me?

Dean: No, I was angry.

It is important to call the patient on his attempt to split hairs and avoid looking at his anger.

RELATIONSHIP WITH PARENTS

Zois: What was her relationship like with your father?

Dean: They had a good relationship.

Zois: How were they towards one another?

Dean: They were each other's best friend. They did a lot of things together. They spent a lot of time with each other.

Zois: Were they affectionate towards one another?

Dean: Yes.

Zois: What would you see between the two of them?

Dean: Hugging and kissing.

Zois: Were you aware that they were having sex?

Dean: Oh, sure.

Zois: How were you aware of it?

Dean: I don't know.

Zois: You say, "Oh sure."

Dean: I was aware of it. If you ask me at what point in life did I become aware of it I can't pinpoint it.

Zois: Yet you were aware that they were having sex?

Dean: Yes.

Zois: How were you aware of it?

Dean: I remember finding prophylactics in my father's dresser.

Zois: Yes.

Dean: At some point in my life, I can't tell you what age, I remember hearing them make love.

Zois: What did you hear?

Dean: Sounds.

Zois: What kind of sounds?

Here again, what follows is an illustration of how the patient would like to avoid dealing with an issue, but with some focusing he begins to recall finding prophylactics in his father's dresser and he goes on to remember hearing them making love. The patient at the beginning of this conversation about the sex life of his parents is not wittingly trying to withhold information. He does not remember it, but with challenge and focus it comes to the surface. However, he is not prepared to give it up completely.

Dean: The sounds of orgasm.

Zois: How do you feel right now?

Dean: Well, you're another one of these assholes, okay.

Zois: You're getting angry with me?

Dean: Well, because you're bothering me.

Zois: I'm bothering you?

Dean: Yes.

Zois: So when I attempt to get into the relationship that you have with your parents you get angry. How angry are you?

Dean: Angry.

Because I am experiencing in the room a very angry person and I am aware that this anger is going to give him difficulty in the transference, I elect to move away from his reaction to sex between his parents and to start to desensitize his ego to the homicidal fantasy impulse. I do that in the standard manner of asking him how angry he is, how he experiences that anger, what he sees in his mind.

DESENSITIZATION OF HOMICIDAL IMPULSE

Zois: How angry? What do you see in your mind?

Dean: Angry enough that the first reaction was to want to kill you.

Zois: What do you see in your mind? How would you do it?

Dean: Well, the building isn't high enough off the ground to do what I told Jacobs I would do, which is to throw him out the window.

Zois: So what would you do?

Dean: But there was something you struck in me and there was something that either came just before it or just after it in terms of tempering the anger.

Zois: I asked you what you saw in your mind.

Dean: You in that closet, hanging up.

Zois: What did I look like?

Dean: Dead.

Zois: What is that like? What do you see? You say I'm hanging there?

Dean: Yeah, you are hanging there.

Zois: What am I hanging by?

Dean: By your neck, something either around it or in it and your head is hanging to the side.

Zois: How do you feel right now physically?

Dean: Fine.

Zois: What are you experiencing?

Dean: Right now, in terms of pain?

Zois: Yes.

Dean: Nothing.

Zois: Emotionally, how do you feel?

Dean: Very uptight.

Zois: *Where do you experience that?*

Dean: Perspiration.

Zois: What else?

Dean: That's it.

TRIANGLE OF PERSONS

Zois: Is this how you felt when you told me that you wanted to kill your mother and your brother?

Dean: No.

Zois: How did you feel when you said that?

Dean: I don't feel anything when I say that.

Zois: How about when you said that he was a pain in your ass all his life?

Dean: It gives me a pain in the ass.

Zois: *Have you thought about him being out of the picture?*

Dean: Oh, sure. He's on borrowed time now.

Zois: What do you picture?

Dean: Nothing.

Zois: You say nothing. You say he's dying?

Dean: Yes.

Zois: So how do you see him dying? Have you thought of it?

Dean: Oh sure.

Zois: You say "sure." You're going back to being general. How do you feel right now?

Dean: Bored.

Zois: You are angry?

Dean: I told you I'm extremely angry.

Zois: And when you got angry with Jacobs you told him you were going to throw him out the window. You told me he was an asshole. Now, what did he do when you told him he was an asshole?

Dean: He got very nervous.

Zois: He said, "I don't want to see you anymore." And you told me I'm an asshole. So what is your goal, that you can defeat the process here?

At this point I have covered some of his feelings toward me in terms of his anger and his homicidal fantasies, and some of the anger towards the people in his current life, his mother and his brother. Then I move to the prior therapist, not so much to discuss the anger but to show the patient how he is using the anger as a self-defeating mechanism, and obviously this has implications for everyone in his life. He has used anger to keep people away from him emotionally. I am also addressing the rage he feels as a defense against intimacy.

Dean: No, I don't want to defeat it.

Zois: Let's look at it. You told Jacobs that he was an

asshole. He didn't want to see you anymore. You felt rejected. So behind all of that anger, there was a rejection.

Dean: Yes.

INTIMACY IN THE TRANSFERENCE

In the following exchange I deal with the intimacy in the transference. I specifically use the phrase "allow me to be useful to you" rather than the phrase "allow me to be close to you" because closeness at this point causes this patient anxiety. It has homosexual implications for him and the reason I elect to do that rather than use a term that will increase his anxiety, such as, "You don't want me to *penetrate* into your life and be close to you," is that I make the assumption that the level of rage as a distancing maneuver is commensurate with the sexual anxiety he has about being close to men. I take this tack, which gets me farther along with a patient that to date has been intractable to treatment, because of his anxiety. I know that the therapist before me was not able to get past the rage and was indeed anxious about the patient's anger or became angry himself. The patient succeeded in defeating him. This is why, in our discussion about the qualifications that a therapist must bring to a treatment, one of them is the ability to tolerate anger and the ability to understand what that anger represents. This is relatively easy in this type of case because he is so angry I do not have much difficulty in ascertaining that the anger was in part a defense and in part rage at the way he had dealt with relationships. I want to stress that it is important to understand the patient's anxiety about intimacy. When you have this kind of a history it is very straightforward and the tack then is to put aside words like "penetrate" and go with the issue of being "useful." Finally, this evaluation illustrates why you must work with the intimacy at all times, even after you have worked with the anger. It is the intimacy that brings about the breakthrough.

To summarize: work with the intimacy and carefully choose the phrases that you are going to use at that point depending on the patient. In a highly resistant, angry patient like this, "useful" is better as a term than "close"; however, at a later point you will want to use the word "close." Just as I desensitized the anger and the homicidal fantasies I have to desensitize the anxiety about intimacy.

Zois: Now here with me, I'm trying to get close to you and ask you these questions and you want to keep me out.

Dean: Wait. Stop for one minute. It's a little bit difficult for me to get as close to you as you might want to get to me in 30 minutes.

Zois: So you rationalize why you should not allow me to be useful to you?

Dean: When they are total strangers to me.

Zois: We're not talking about that.

Dean: That's what you are.

Zois: We're not talking about that. We're talking about you being afraid of letting people get close to you. Is that true or not?

Dean: I think that there's not just one answer to it. There are many people who I have allowed to get very close to me.

Zois: Who is close to you?

Dean: There are many people that I allow to get close to me.

Zois: Name them.

Dean: I have a very few—

Zois: Who is close to you?

Dean: I have a few very close friends. I have allowed a few women to get very close to me.

Zois: Yet you say you have defeated relationships?

Dean: Yes.

Zois: You have reported to me that when you have certain feelings you don't deal with them directly, they make you very anxious, so you distance yourself. You were angry with your girlfriend last night, so you left. You were angry with your mother, so you didn't call her. You didn't want to deal with it. With the first doctor, whose name you can't remember, who you liked, who didn't take you into treatment, when you called him up there was the rationalization that it was for a list.

Dean: Yes.

Zois: You tend to put a wall up around yourself.

Dean: Okay.

Zois: Is that so?

Dean: Yes.

Zois: And in here, when I'm talking to you and I start to ask you questions, you put a wall up and you get angry and you want to defeat the process. You want to kill me off.

Dean: Okay.

Zois: We see the evidence. You are calling me names in the same way you were calling Jacobs names and he got rid of you and you felt hurt.

Dean: I don't feel hurt.

Zois: You say you felt rejected. You were surprised when he called.

Dean: No, I said I don't feel hurt by anything that you've said.

Zois: You feel angry.

Dean: Yes.

Zois: You're trying to kill me off?

Dean: I haven't even tried to.

Zois: Sure you have.

Dean: No.

Zois: Yes you have. I asked you questions. You censor yourself. You get irritated, then you tell me I'm an asshole, when 15 minutes ago you told me what result that has gotten you from other therapists. He cut you off. So you had the thought that you shouldn't see me again.

Dean: No.

Zois: You didn't? You told me you were angry, you are bored, I'm an asshole and furthermore you are telling me the last time you called someone else an asshole he got rid of you.

Dean: Are you trying to tell me something?

Zois: What is that?

AMBIVALENCE AND THE IMPULSE TO CONTINUE IN THE OLD WAY

Dean: What, that you don't feel that this process will work for me? Is that what you are trying to tell me?

Zois: I'm trying to tell you that you have systematically tried to defeat yourself through your life.

Dean: I agree with you.

Zois: I see it here.

Dean: I'm very self-destructive.

Zois: How did we jump from that to you saying I don't want to treat you anymore? That's your thought?

Dean: Well, I'm just trying to save both of us a lot of time and effort, if that's the conclusion you are coming to.

Zois: These are the words you want from my mouth?

Dean: I wouldn't be here if those are the words I want to hear.

Zois: On the one hand, you come here of your own free will.

Dean: Yes.

Zois: On the other hand, we see here and in your

personal life and with other therapists, there is a part of you that wants to take revenge on yourself.

Dean: I agree with that totally.

Zois: That's what's going on right now.

Dean: Okay.

Zois: So you have the idea that this might not work for you and that I should tell you.

Dean: Well, I hope that it will work for me.

Zois: We see in the past you have defeated yourself, and as I ask you questions about this intense relationship that you have with your mother, you get very angry, and you deal with that anger by becoming anxious, by becoming sarcastic, by trying to provoke me. *Do you do that to other people?*

Dean: Yes.

Zois: So it's a familiar scenario?

Dean: Yes. Unfortunately, it's true.

Zois: That's what's going on here now.

Dean: If I say to you what comes into my mind, then your answer will be, because you are—

Zois: You want to censor yourself?

Dean: No, it isn't a question of censoring myself.

Zois: What's on your mind?

Dean: Maybe that's the way I have behaved for all of this period of time and I suspect that it just doesn't change instantaneously.

Zois: Who is talking about instant change? You feel I am attacking you?

Dean: Do I feel attacked? No.

Zois: Do you feel accused?

Dean: Absolutely not.

Zois: So why are you defending yourself? That's what you're doing, isn't it?

Dean: No. I'm trying to explain something to you.

Zois: You're explaining your behavior to me.

Dean: Okay.

Zois: Now, is that familiar to you in your past?

Dean: Absolutely.

Zois: Defending yourself?

Dean: Yes.

Zois: Who else do you explain yourself to besides me?

Dean: Whoever I got myself in trouble with.

Zois: Who would you have the trouble with?

Dean: My mother, my girlfriends, my partners, whoever.

Zois: You would find yourself explaining yourself to these people?

Dean: Yeah. I can bullshit pretty well.

Zois: How do you feel that you have to explain yourself?

Dean: If it gets me off the hook, it's okay.

Zois: How do you feel towards the people that you have to explain yourself to?

Dean: I feel like I've conned them.

Zois: How do you feel right now?

Dean: This second, pretty good.

Zois: Okay. We'll take a five-minute break and then we'll continue the evaluation.

It is obvious from my tone and the questions that I am asking that I believe that I have made progress in breaking through the patient's defenses. I cover a lot of ground in terms of bringing the patient to an awareness of how self-destructive his behavior is and how he has tried to bankrupt his life. He has systematically tried to defeat the therapist and we see very clearly that the patient is very ambivalent indeed about leaving the self-destructive part of his behavior behind. This is because the guilt that causes that self-destructiveness has not been processed or resolved. This degree of ambivalence tells us that he is not going to see the light in one session. We know that he has too many angry and sadistic impulses toward his parents, his brother, and other people in his past and current life; and because these impulses are so deeply rooted he will not be able to give them up easily. The guilt generates the ambivalence in him. However, having said that, I see that he is a good candidate for this therapy because he can become emotionally comfortable with me in the room. His anger has dissipated, his anxiety has diminished, he is able to make connections, and that is why I am able to move quickly to help him understand his anger is a defense against pain and hurt when I talk about how he felt rejected by the therapist who refused to see him.

Whenever the evaluation exceeds one hour, I always ask the patient to reflect on the session after the break is taken. If the evaluation ends without an intermission I ask this question toward the end:

Zois: Can you tell me your impression of our talk here so far today as you compare it to other therapy you've had?

Dean: I've never been involved with any kind of confrontation. Jacobs minimally. So this was a brand new ball game to me. It became obvious to me that there are certain things that I'm aware of that I've been hiding behind that are not only obvious to me, but they must be obvious to other people, not only trained psychiatrists, but just regular people, in terms of overweight, anger and things of that sort. Do I think it can work for me? Yeah, I think so, because it's the kind of challenge I need. I need to be confronted. I need to run into somebody who won't let me get away with any of my shit.

Zois: Are you saying, in that sense, it's different for you here?

Dean: Totally different.

Zois: You say it came to mind that there are certain things that you do?

Dean: I didn't realize, as an example, however I answer a question, whether it be as sharply focused as some of the ones that you were asking, but as I was doing it, I became totally aware of how many times I'm tempted to or my speech pattern or brain pattern or whatever it is will answer a question without really answering it by using any one of a series of adjectives. Whether it's "I think," "possibly," "probably," or "maybe," or that kind of thing. It became apparent that there were a number of times where it was about to flow out of my mouth and I was going to say I caught myself, I became conscious of it. Then when I was sitting out there, I said "Why?" What has that done for me historically? Is that protective?

Zois: Can you tell me about your relationships? How old were you when you got married?

Dean: Twenty-eight.

Zois: How long had you known your wife?

Dean: A year.

Zois: Was that the first serious relationship that you had?

Dean: No.

Zois: What was the relationship prior to that?

Dean: A gal in college, really serious, I thought I was going to marry her.

Zois: How old were you when you started dating?

Dean: Thirteen, 14, I guess.

Zois: How old were you when you had intercourse?

Dean: College.

Zois: Was it with the girl that you were serious with?

Dean: No, before that.

Zois: How long was the relationship with this girl in college?

Dean: Pretty close to three years, I guess.

Zois: How did it end?

Dean: I didn't want to get married. Oh, I don't know if it's important or not, but I had a very unusual sexual relationship when I was quite a young child.

Zois: How old?

Dean: Three. We had a European housekeeper who must have been a sicko and she used to sleep in my room and for quite a long period of time, I'm not sure how long, but at least a year or so, I was her lover at 3 years old.

Zois: How old was she?

Dean: In her twenties.

Zois: What would transpire between the two of you?

Dean: Oral intercourse, whatever a 3-year-old can do.

Zois: This lasted for about a year?

Dean: It may have been longer, I'm not sure.

Zois: Where was your brother at that time when you were 3? Where was he sleeping?

Dean: In the same room.

Zois: Was he aware of what was going on?

Dean: I don't believe so. It was something we never discussed.

Zois: Did she have any sexual encounters with your brother?

Dean: Not that I know of, but this goes back and this has given me an abnormal sexual desire, an appetite my whole life.

Zois: When you say that, can you describe what you mean?

Dean: I mean at times I'm totally consumed by sex.

Zois: What is that like for you? What happens?

Dean: It's a high. I just want to screw all day long and all night long.

Zois: Under what circumstances do you?

Dean: Certain women. I can go from here and decide to get laid on the way back to my office, a girl I lived with for a while, I would stop at her office, go in and close the door, screw her and then go on back downtown.

The patient is giving a description of one of the ways he deals with anxiety and pressure, which is to act out sexually. He is not aware of this; instead, he rationalizes that his frenetic sexual activity arises from a relationship he had with a babysitter at a very early age.

Zois: Have you done things with her before?

Dean: Constantly.

Zois: How about when you were married? How was that for you?

Dean: I think, if I recall, I got married in July and I first started screwing around in November and never stopped.

SEXUAL HISTORY

Zois: When you would have intercourse with your wife, what would be your sexual fantasies?

Dean: During intercourse?

Zois: Yes.

Dean: None.

Zois: When you were having intercourse you had no thoughts?

Dean: No, but I suspect, I know this gal that I was referring to before, her name was Lizzie. I have no idea what her last name was. I believe that I have spent the rest of my life looking all over the world for her. All the girls I have been involved with have looked like her.

Zois: What did she look like?

Dean: Long blond hair, thin but extremely well built.

Zois: When you masturbate, what would your sexual fantasies be?

Dean: Lizzie.

Zois: Up to what age?

Dean: I don't know.

Zois: How about now, what are your sexual fantasies?

Dean: All over the lot.

Zois: All over the lot doesn't tell me anything.

Dean: I fantasized about having oral sex with her.

Zois: What do you see in your mind?

Dean: She having oral sex with me and me having oral sex with her.

OEDIPAL TRIANGLES (CONTINUED)

Zois: Who else do you fantasize about?

Dean: A friend of my mother's that I had an affair with.

Zois: How old was she?

Dean: She's a number of years younger than my mother. I would imagine that she's 70 today.

Zois: She was a friend of your mother's?

Dean: Yes. She and her husband were my parents' closest friends.

Zois: This affair was after your father died?

Dean: Yes.

Zois: They were close friends of your parents?

Dean: Very close friends.

Zois: How did the affair come about?

Dean: I used to play golf with her husband and one Saturday or Sunday we played golf. I don't remember, but I have the feeling that my mother was away or something and I went back to their house and we were all lying on the living room floor watching television and I touched her. And that was how it started. And I went on like that apparently.

Zois: Was her husband aware?

Dean: I don't believe so.

Zois: Did you ever tell your mother about that?

Dean: No.

Zois: Did you ever tell her about Lizzie?

Dean: I never told her about it, but somehow they found out.

Zois: How did you know that?

Dean: She just disappeared very quickly and I seem to have a recollection of something that happened. I mean, I can't pin it down and say I'm positive of it, but it's pretty clear in my mind.

Zois: Did your mother ever discuss this with you?

Dean: No. The recollection is of standing in the kitchen and there were other women there and I came over and put my arms around somebody's leg and put my hand right up her skirt and this poor woman must have screamed bloody murder. Now, if there was conversation I don't remember, maybe that's the beginning of my successfully avoiding issues.

Zois: So you and your mother never discussed it?

Dean: No, I'm not saying that. If we did, I have no recollection of it. I recall that one other incident.

Zois: You recall the instance, but you don't recall your mother and you talking about it?

Dean: No.

Zois: How about your father?

Dean: No.

Zois: Was there ever a time in your life when you were seeing only one woman?

Dean: Would you qualify time? How long a time?

Zois: Was there any period of time in your mind?

Dean: A week, a month, six months, a year.

Zois: Was there any sustained amount of time?

Dean: Yeah. It was probably about a year with a girlfriend, Tracy, that I was not fooling around with anyone else. There was never any time with another girlfriend, Sue, that I wasn't fooling around. There has never been any period of time with Kim, my current girlfriend, that I haven't fooled around.

Zois: So is it accurate to say that you've never been able to commit yourself to one woman?

Dean: That is totally accurate.

Zois: This sexual behavior that you describe is part of that?

Dean: Yes.

Zois: When you were angry with Kim you had two sexual fantasies. One is a woman who works for you and the other one, this friend of your mother's?

Dean: Yes.

Zois: Do you find that when you get angry at Kim—

Dean: Sex.

Zois: Sex with other women?

Dean: Even with the woman I'm angry with, that would relieve some of the emotional tension.

Zois: So sex is one way you deal with your anxiety?

Dean: I hadn't thought of it that way but when you say it, it sounds right.

Zois: Getting back to your fantasies, are there ever more than two people in the fantasy?

Dean: Yeah, I have a burning desire, but I've never had a ménage à trois.

Zois: Does that come to mind when you are having sex?

Dean: Not that I can recall.

Zois:Is there ever a woman in the fantasy that you can't identify?

Dean: No, but there is a recurrent dream that I have had. I haven't had it recently, but I used to have it all the time and there was both a male and a female in it that were faceless.

Zois: What would go on in the dream?

Dean: Well, part of it that comes to me immediately is that there is a long flight of steps and there is a room that is so vague, it's kind of just shadows and light. And, interestingly enough, a couple of years ago I was looking for a painting and I met a young artist whose work I liked and he was showing me canvases and there was this painting that just totally fit. It was that room and that dream. It looked as if it had one whole wall of doors. I have it; it was almost a compulsion to buy it.

Zois: So in the dream there is a long flight of stairs and a room with light and shadows. What else was in the room.

Dean: Nothing.

Zois: And the man and the woman?

Dean: The man was my father. That much I once worked out, and the woman I have no idea.

Zois: Where were they in the dream? What were they doing?

Dean: He was walking. He was further up the stairs than I was and she was behind me. That is what comes to my mind right now. My gut tells me that she is Lizzie.

Zois: What would transpire in the dream?

Dean: I don't know.

Zois: It was a recurring dream you had frequently about you and this man and this woman walking up a flight of stairs?

Dean: In this room with the doors and just shadow and light.

Zois: Were there any other objects in the room?

Dean: No.

Zois: How big was the room?

Dean: It's not that kind of perspective. My perspective of it would be, I'm only looking at a portion of it.

Zois: What would go on in the room?

Dean: No recall.

Zois: Did the two people enter the room with you when you walk up the stairs?

Dean: I don't know.

Zois: How were you feeling in that dream when it happened?

Dean: It's been a long time. I don't know.

Zois: You say that you worked out that that man was your father?

Dean: You know what, I take it back. I had that dream recently. Within the last few months and as I'm sitting here there are things that become so clear to me that night and I've totally put them aside.

Zois: How do you feel right now?

Dean: Very relaxed.

When exploring a dream, elicit as much detail as possible. You should have the patient repeat the dream. During this process ask about the emotional tone of the dream. "What was the feeling in the dream? How do you feel right now as you think of it?" I have gained valuable information about the patient's incest impulses. Lizzie, his mother's "friend," and the faceless woman in the dream are representations of his mother. The fantasy or dream of a faceless person is common. The technical response is: "You have a dream of having sex with a woman, but you don't want to know who she is. You don't give her a face." I also file away for future reference his sadistic impulses towards men. He had sex with the wife of a man he plays golf with, who is also his father's friend.

At this point I elect to gather more history.

ALCOHOL AND DRUG HISTORY

Zois: At the beginning of our interview you talked about having these physical episodes.

Dean: Just one.

Zois: When was that?

Dean: April 8th.

Zois: Where were you when you had it?

Dean: I was at a very good friend's house at a party. I had a couple of drinks. I was not drunk. I wasn't on any other drugs. I had gotten a plate of food and opened up the sliding doors to go out on the patio and that's all I remember. By the time I came to I felt fine.

Zois: When did you come to? Were you at home or at the hospital?

Dean: Right there on the ground. My former wife was able to get in touch with my internist and they took me to the hospital where I spent the next four days. I had every test and they found absolutely nothing.

Zois: How do you feel about that experience? What is your thought?

Dean: I was quite frightened.

Zois: How do you feel about it now?

Dean: Nothing at all. If I did I wouldn't smoke or drink or be overweight.

Zois: How much do you drink?

I question the amount he drinks because he may have described an alcoholic blackout.

Dean: It depends. A lot.

Zois: Do you drink every day?

Dean: No.

Zois: Do you consider it a problem for you?

Dean: No.

Zois: Do you drink until you are intoxicated?

Dean: I never get intoxicated.

Zois: You say a lot?

Dean: If I start at noon I can drink until two-thirty, three o'clock in the morning. I do a fair amount of entertaining at lunchtime. But as a conscious effort I try not to drink during the day. I'm at a point in my life where I just don't need it.

Zois: Do you use anything else? Do you take drugs of any kind?

Dean: No.

Zois: So there is nothing else besides drinking?

Dean: I was a Tylenol freak for a long time.

Zois: You say you had this physical episode, these pains in your back, neck, and rectal area?

Dean: Neck, shoulder.

Zois: Neck, back, shoulder, and rectal area?

Dean: Yes.

Zois: What other problems do you have?

Dean: In terms of?

Zois: Whatever comes to mind.

Dean: Bad headaches.

Zois: How often do you get those?

Dean: A lot, almost every day.

AREAS OF DISTURBANCE (CONTINUED)

Zois: What other problems do you have?

Dean: I do not sleep.

Zois: How long has that been going on?

Dean: Twenty-five years. I can sleep at any time except in bed at night.

Zois: Do you have difficulty going to sleep or do you wake up early?

Dean: I can fall asleep at will almost any time, but I'll only sleep for a short period of time. The last few months, well, last night I got into bed at eleven and was wide awake still at four.

Zois: What other problems do you have?

Dean: I'm not happy.

Zois: When you say that what are you describing?

Dean: I suppose that I have what most people in the world would think would be the basis of some kind of happiness: pretty successful, I have a good business, I have two super kids, I can afford to do almost anything I want in this world. I just don't have peace of mind.

Zois: Could you be specific?

Dean: I don't know how to be any more specific than that.

Zois: Describe that.

Dean: I would like to be very much in love with somebody and trust them, which I can't, I don't. Not that I don't love someone, I just can't trust them. I would like to have somebody as a best friend.

Zois: Is there anybody there?

Dean: I think Kim could be. It's not her fault, it's mine.

Zois: You had the thought that you don't have a best friend and that you are unable to be close to somebody.

Dean: No. I think if I've led you to that conclusion that's not—

Zois: You say, "I don't have a best friend," and "I don't interest anybody enough that I can be in love with them. I can love but I can't get close." Those are your words. Is that true?

Dean: Maybe it's truer than I would like to think.

Zois: It's something that you don't want to look at?

Dean: Absolutely.

Zois: But if you are able to be honest with yourself that's how you feel?

Dean: Yes.

ISOLATION

Zois: You feel alone?

Dean: I don't know. I'm not sure. If there's a difference between being alone and feeling alone then I accept that.

Zois: There are people around you?

Dean: Yes.

Zois: And by your description you can get many people around you?

Dean: Snapping my fingers, yeah.

Zois: But you feel alone?

Dean: Yeah, even with many people around me.

Zois: You shut them out.

Dean: Yes.

Again the emphasis is on what the patient has done to others, not what others have done to him. There is no value in reinforcing the individual's impulse to assume the role of victim. The tendency for patients to do this is universal.

ANXIETY ABOUT INTIMACY

Zois: You can't get close to someone?

Dean: Yes.

Zois: How do you feel when you think about that?

Dean: Pained.

Zois: What's that like right now?

Dean: It's a sense of failure.

Zois: What's the emotion? Do you feel tearful as you think about that?

Dean: No.

Zois: How do you feel?

Dean: Numb. I don't feel anything.

Zois: So you guard against those feelings?

Dean: If that's the opposite to having a feeling, then yeah.

Zois: Let's look at what you said. When you are feeling unhappy or alone or you are anxious you feel a sexual desire.

Dean: Yeah.

Zois: You distance yourself from those feelings in that way. You use sex to keep away from those feelings of being cut off?

Dean: I don't have a better answer, but I wouldn't reject it.

Zois: As you were sitting here and talking about some things, you had a thought that you could stop off before the office, for instance?

Dean: Yes.

Zois: So?

Dean: So that's fulfillment of the emotional pain that's created here—I'll get rid of it by getting laid on the way back to the office.

Zois: This is how you tell me you try to handle it, is that correct so far?

Dean: Yeah. The process probably was that was what was going through my mind at that particular moment. If it's really bad here for this period of time I'll make it feel good by stopping off for a quickie.

Zois: That's generally how it's been most of your life?

Dean: Yes, either that or party and have a big meal and have fun.

Zois: How do you feel right now?

Dean: Pretty comfortable.

Zois: How do you feel about undergoing this kind of therapy?

Dean: Well, I said to you before, it's so totally different, but I'm having tremendous pain in my chest right now.

Zois: You smile when you say that.

Dean: Well, because it's obvious you asked a question and I get the pain as I start to answer the question. The smile is the connection of putting them all together. It's a brand new concept, but I can see that it appears to work. I've become aware of some things in this short period of time that are fascinating. You force the issue or the process forces the issues and you lead the process.

At the end of the initial interview, I have arrived at a psychodynamic formulation. I share this information with the patient in a straightforward way:

SUMMATION

Zois: We see that you have a tendency to be a self-sabotaging individual. You attempted to do it here with me several times during our evaluation. And you have done it in your life. You are still plagued by your father's death. That guilt has never been resolved. You have never said goodbye to your father. We have seen that you have a tendency to want to perpetuate your guilt, by defeating the therapy, by not allowing people to be useful to you. You have a need to suffer. You jeopardize your work, you jeopardize your relationships. Your guilt about your father's death has been baggage you've carried with you. You have attempted to use rage, anger, and drinking to screw up everything in your life that is of value. You have tried to do it here with me. Now the question is, what are you going to do about it? Today we have touched on these issues. Do you believe that this form of therapy will be useful to you?

Dean: Yes.

Zois: Why?

Dean: I've learned a lot of things that I never thought of before.

Zois: This is true. But we've seen there are significant issues in your life that you'll need to overcome and clarify. Do you agree with that?

Dean: Yes.

This sets the tone for the therapy. The patient knows he must commit and be an active participant in the therapy.

Zois: How do you feel about going through this?

Dean: I would like to, very much.

The session is concluded.

Toward the end of the interview we see that the patient is in touch with tender and sad feelings. He handles his emotions very differently than when he began the session. He is able to make connections. He is relating to me without the degree of defensiveness that he was using at the outset. The defenses of anger, generalization, vagueness, and rationalization are not present. He has made progress and he is viewing old issues in a new way.

6

Resistance

Resistance and the defenses it engenders constitute the patient's main hindrance to improvement. All patients come to therapy with some degree of resistance. It is in addressing resistance that the ST technique has its greatest efficacy.

Resistance is initiated by the patient to protect the deep secrets, the pain, grief, shame, and guilt that lie within the psyche. Throughout the therapy, defenses will be marshaled. Hopefully those defenses will be exhausted by the therapist. However, it is a continuous struggle. When each subject or conflict for the patient is touched on, anxiety will engender more resistance. We have to disabuse ourselves of the notion that once we have dealt with the defenses on one issue that they are not going to recur. Therapists have to appreciate the frequency with which they can recur, and not become discouraged. The reappearance of defenses does not mean progress is not being made.

EXAMPLES OF RESISTANCE, FROM MODERATE TO SEVERE

It is helpful to assign a 1 to 10 point value to resistance. There is no such thing as zero resistance. 1+ resistance would be generalized defenses of vagueness: "I think," "I guess," "maybe." Resistance that is a little more accentuated would be the defense of helplessness: "I don't know." A more moderate to severe defense would be weepiness: the "wall of water" to keep the therapist out, or anger as a defense against looking at material. The most severe defense would be a direct refusal to discuss an issue. It is useful when doing an interview to assign a point value to the resistance. Resistance waxes and wanes. Do not have the expectation that confronting resistance ensures its disappearance. A patient will manifest significant resistance, you will break through, you will exhaust those defenses, and a session or two later, or perhaps in the same session, you may see the same intensity of resistance manifest itself again.

RESISTANCE AS A WAY TO SABOTAGE THE THERAPY

The patient who constantly uses the defense of helplessness by saying "I don't know" is expressing passivity and irritation toward the therapist. Frequently the therapist will become frustrated and begin to intellectualize to the patient. The patient is continually inviting the therapist to give direction and explanations. The classic statement from the patient after the therapist has made an interpretation is, "I understand this, Doctor, but it doesn't help me." That statement can cause the therapist to accept the invitation to intellectualize and become didactic in attempting to explain to the patient why it should help. It is a mistake to fall into this trap. What is important is to make the interpretation of the passivity of that defense. The reply should be, "Do you notice how when I ask you a question or when I make an interpretation you become passive? You are passive as a function of your irritation toward me, that I am trying to penetrate into your life. You tell me you understand it but you cannot do anything about it. How do you feel when you become passive like this with me here in the room?" The next question should be, "Do you do this with other people?" Notice again we are working with the triangle of the therapist, the current people, and the past people, in terms of dealing with the impulse/feeling, the anxiety, and the defense engendered by the interaction. By doing this, the therapist stays within the framework of what is therapeutic, rather than falling into the quagmire of intellectualizing and attempting to "teach" the patient, which allows the patient to gain control of the therapy. The therapy then degenerates into an intellectualized interaction where the patient has "trained" the therapist to expect the patient to come in and report a dilemma, a problem, or a situation, and sit back and wait for the therapist to give advice.

Unfortunately this happens more often than it should. We have to keep in mind the etiology of it. We see the therapist being disarmed by resistance in the form of intellectualization and then being seduced into a nontherapeutic stance. The therapist who does this runs the risk of conducting a therapy that has no substance to it, that only ameliorates issues in a superficial way and for only a brief period of time.

Other ways that resistance can sabotage therapy are more blatant and dramatic. An obvious form of sabotage is the patient who comes in after a session or so and announces to the therapist that he or she has feelings toward the therapist or who invites the therapist to have a relationship. There are many others: coming late to sessions, having constant problems about working out a fee schedule, making excuses for canceling sessions. All of these are forms of resistance that have to be addressed directly.

7

Transference

Patients come to therapy with strong feelings about the important people, past and present, in their lives. They then transfer those feelings to the therapist. In essence they confuse the therapist with significant others and react to the therapist accordingly. The examination of this *neurotic transference* allows patients to work through their conflicts. Authentic feelings, sometimes tender, are also engendered toward the therapist for trying to help them. It is important to keep that distinction in mind because much of the material that manifests itself in the latter part of the therapy can be the result of authentic feelings that are not part of the neurotic transference.

THE CORRELATION BETWEEN TRANSFERENCE AND INTIMACY

The cornerstone of a successful therapy is the ability of the therapist to work with the intimacy in the transference. Working with the intimacy in the transference implies bringing to the patient's awareness the emotions engendered toward the therapist because he is attempting to be useful. Accomplishing intimacy in the transference is, in my mind, the paramount issue in any therapy.

Most people who have difficulty being intimate feel a lack of entitlement. For them it is easier to give than receive. A lack of entitlement is another reason patients attempt to keep a wall between themselves and the therapist.

THE PARAMOUNT ROLE OF INTIMACY IN ACHIEVING A SUCCESSFUL THERAPEUTIC OUTCOME

The ability to work with the intimacy is one of the most effective means of dealing with the patient's guilt and lack of entitlement. I cannot stress enough that in my twenty-five years of doing therapy, working with the intimacy has enabled me, in the majority of cases, to bring about the kind of change that the patient has been seeking.

In order to achieve intimacy in the transference, the therapist has to break through the wall of defenses that the patient has erected. That wall exists, to varying degrees, around everybody. This is an evolutionary process. You do not break through, accomplish intimacy, and then it is written in stone forever. Having success in breaking through does not mean that the patient is not going to seal over again. All it means is that the seal will not be as impermeable to challenge as it was the first time.

The other hallmark of this therapy is repetition. The therapist should not be discouraged because defenses continuously return. The goal is that the intensity and duration of those defenses will diminish over time.

On reviewing tapes of patients that have not progressed as well as they could have, the criticism I have had of my work was my not sufficiently working with the intimacy. When I first began, much of the work I was doing focused around the anger that arose when the defenses were challenged. By focusing on the anger, my goal was to desensitize the patient to rageful impulses in the transference. While working with the anger is an important component of therapy, I came to realize that working only with the anger did not achieve the result I had hoped for. Solely focusing on negative emotions is an incomplete therapy that supports the sense of victimization. Working with the intimacy in the transference is where I have achieved my most effective breakthroughs and had my most positive outcomes.

COUNTERTRANSFERENCE: THE CORRELATION BETWEEN COUNTERTRANSFERENCE AND THE PATIENT'S RESISTANCE

In order to do this type of therapy effectively, the therapist has to evaluate his or her own reaction to anger and intimacy. There will be times during treatment that the therapist is experiencing the same psychological issues as the patient. If the therapist has anxiety about anger and cannot tolerate people being angry at him, then the therapist is going to have a difficult time eliciting the anger and rage that is stored up in the patient. The same holds true for intimacy. Some therapists fear they are going to lose patients if they upset them, but in truth the reverse happens. The patient forms a strong connection with a therapist who is active. The patient acknowledges, "This person is willing to face the truth together with me." The therapist is communicating to the patient in the same way that the patient is communicating to the therapist, both covertly and overtly. In many instances a patient will pick up on the therapist's anxiety about anger or intimacy and will spare the therapist.

The hope is that the therapist has a greater awareness and a better handle on his or her own neurotic tendencies. To assume that therapists do not have any shortcomings ranges somewhere from silly to grandiose. This is another reason why videotaping is so important. It not only teaches us about the patients and the technique, it gives us insight into our own frailties and vulnerabilities.

Vigilance in doing therapy applies not only to what the patient is saying but also to how the therapist is responding. This issue also holds true for sexual impulses. A trainee I was supervising was confronted with a very attractive patient. In the supervision it was pointed out that he was staying away from the anger in the patient and avoiding sexual issues. He recalled at that point that during the therapy he had fantasized about the patient undressing. He realized that he was not dealing with the anger because he wanted the patient to like him. He was able to go back to the interview and complete the evaluation effectively.

To summarize the key issues of this section: (1) always work with the intimacy in the transference, and (2) always be vigilant about your own reactions. The therapist has nothing to be embarrassed about in admitting his or her own vulnerabilities.

The following vignette from Dean's fourth session illustrates some of the ways technically that we help the patient allow the therapist to get close. If we can accomplish intimacy in the transference, then this will enable the patient to become intimate with other people. There is nothing more educative and useful than what is accomplished in the transference. This illustration serves to demonstrate how resistance can be dealt with in the transference by interpreting the patient's distancing and self-sabotage. Technically in the session I want to keep stressing his anxiety and his self sabotage in blocking me from getting close to him or being useful to him. This patient comes in enraged at the world and at me as the therapist. He gives a history of ragefulness at preceding therapists. In this session, Dean relates his anger toward his father for an episode that occurred when Dean was 12. I attempt to deal with that anger and come up against a wall. When I shift gears and focus on the intimacy the result, as we will see, is startling.

Zois: How did you feel when your father kicked you?

Dean: Angry.

Zois: How angry were you with him?

Dean: I don't know; no recollection.

Zois: What told you that you were angry?

Dean: I'm telling you now, that's all.

Zois: You say your mother came to the room and got in between the two of you?

Dean: My recall is that he was trying to get me in a corner somewhere, I think in the bathroom and she somehow got between us and I was on the floor in the corner and he kicked me.

Zois: Where did he kick you?

Dean: In my leg, I seem to recall.

Zois: How do you feel now as you look back on that?

Dean: I am very unhappy about discussing it. Now get off it, okay?

Zois: It makes you very sad?

Dean: I said get off it [angrily].

Zois: Now you want me to get off it?

Dean: No, I don't want you to, I'm telling you to.

Zois: So you provoke me. You come here, you spend all this time, you spend your money, and a part of you wants to keep punishing yourself. What will happen if we "get off it"? You will go on with these feelings. I'll be useless to you. You will be there behind your wall. You won't show me your feelings and you'll leave here unhappy, a pained person and you are very sad now and you are fighting hard to hold back that sadness and you are trying to keep me away from it by getting angry with me, by being provocative. So that you, in your account, will drive me away. As you drive everybody else away. I can afford to fail but you can't.

Making this statement is important because it demonstrates to the patient that I am not impervious to his ability to defeat me. This cuts across the neurotic grain because the patient's desire to see me as omnipotent and omniscient serves another goal, which is to let me do the work. This position then reinforces the defense of passivity, which is, in essence, that no work shall be done. When I make the statement "I can afford to fail" I am addressing that issue and putting the responsibility onto the individual to do the work. This interpretation brings about a dramatic change at this point.

Dean: You make it sound like it is so easy for it just to come out [affect soft; anger subsides].

Zois: And it's not?

Dean: You better believe it.

Zois: But you're fighting very hard to hold it in.

Dean: You bet your sweet bippie it's tough.

Zois: You are fighting very hard to hold it in and you've done that all of your life.

Dean: Are you capable of understanding that the words just won't come out?

Zois: So it's very painful for you sitting here right now?

Dean: It's extremely painful and it's very sad.

Zois: How sad is it?

Dean: As sad as I've been in a long time [patient appears sad].

When a patient is reluctant or refuses to discuss a painful subject, always move to the intimacy in the transference. This enabled Dean to free himself from the defensive rage that he was using to keep a distance from me.

In the next session he was a changed man. For the past week he was in touch with the sadness and pain he had spent a lifetime avoiding.

Zois: What are your thoughts?

Dean: I find things are happening. Last week we talked about sadness and crying and you asked me a number of questions and before the night was over I was crying and in pain. What's going on? Is this part of the process? Is this the power of suggestion? I want to know.

Zois: What happened last week after you left here?

Dean: Is your question avoidance of answering my question or are we going to try to work it out and find out?

Zois: Let's clarify to see what happened to get an idea of what it's all about.

Dean: Okay. A tremendous feeling of weight on my chest.

Zois: When was that?

Dean: Right now sitting outside. I got here a few minutes early and I walked around and passed a funeral parlor, and I got a scary feeling.

Zois: What was the thought you had as you walked by the funeral parlor?

Dean: There was a hearse parked on the street and I got the feeling that that's where they put bodies and there was an overwhelming feeling of anxiety.

Zois: When you left here last week you say—

Dean: I went back to my office and everything was fine. I left there and met Kim at my apartment. We went to the theater and enjoyed it. Went out for dinner after and enjoyed it and I was pretty uptight, but I felt okay. We talked for a while after we got in bed and I started crying.

Zois: What were you talking about?

Dean: Some parts of what had gone on here.

Zois: What were you talking about?

Dean: I made the observation about punishment for telling the truth. She asked me an interesting question. She said, "Were you an abused child?" And I said, "I don't know." And then in the course of the conversation she said, "We talked about many things over the time that we've known each other. We've never talked about your father at all."

She said the closest that we ever came to it was about a month ago when a close friend of mine from out of town came to visit and we had dinner. He and I grew up together from little kids until we went to college and then there was a period of 20 years we never saw each other. One night a few years ago he called and now whenever he's in town we see each other. I asked him what his recollection of my father was. He made some comments that I don't even remember what they were, but I would not say that I particularly agreed with him. Some I didn't disagree with either.

Zois: You say you didn't remember what he said?

Dean: And Kim reminded me that was the only time. Out of nowhere she asked the question about was

I an abused child. As I remember that was the point at which I started getting very teary and I got very, very anxious. I couldn't even stay in bed. I got up and started walking up and down my bedroom. I'm not sure about the use of the term "abuse." Does that mean physical abuse only?

Zois: What comes to mind?

Dean: Well, as I began to think about it, I can't say other than that incident, although I'm sure there were others, where I might have been physically abused, but somehow I feel that I was mentally abused. It seemed obvious to me that my brother was my mother's favorite and I recall that I was always getting chewed out because he was such a great student and I was such a fuck-up. I remember I was in grammar school and we got caught smoking and got kicked out of school. I'm sure I must have gotten a lot of shit for that. I say "I'm sure" but if you say specifically, I remember nothing. Then Kim asked if my father abused my mother. I said, "Not that I'm aware of." But I was sad and I have been since our session last week. I just feel heavy. On Sunday, whatever it is, it seemed to come in waves. It's overwhelming. I can't specifically say that it's this or that.

Zois: What were your thoughts Sunday?

Dean: I don't know.

Zois: Where were you?

Dean: I had gone for a long walk, alone, at the ocean. I walked a few miles and I could feel this sadness. That's all I could feel and I really wanted to cry as I was walking. It was one crazy thought that came into my mind: Twenty-some-odd years ago a close friend that lived in the same apartment complex had gone on vacation and they brought presents for my wife and son but not a goddamn thing for me. And I remember crying. I remember telling my wife that the woman was a bitch. That's pretty dumb, I realize.

Zois: You're calling yourself names but the feeling is there.

Dean: Yes.

Zois: How do you feel now as you think about it?

Dean: I feel like an ass for even saying it to you because it's such a stupid thing, but it must have evoked a tremendous—

Zois: What does it evoke now?

Dean: Nothing.

Zois: You look upset but you are also concerned about my reaction.

Dean: Not consciously.

Zois: You say, "I feel like an ass telling you that."

Dean: Because it is a waste of time to tell you something, but with the thought that it must have invoked a re-awakening of a similar kind of feeling for something that happened at some other time when somebody didn't bring me something, my parents or someone. I don't know. That's what my head tells me.

Zois: The idea of being left out, rejected, fills you with a real sadness, to the point that you cried.

Dean: Yes.

Zois: In here as you tell me about it, on the one hand, you are experiencing that feeling. On the other hand, you are having difficulty in telling me that feeling and you think to yourself that showing me the feeling—

Dean: You mean to cry in here?

Zois: Do you experience the sadness? You say to yourself you must be an ass in my eyes, which is a distancing thought.

Dean: I don't buy that, but it could be.

Zois: On the one hand, you are recording what happened. On the other hand, you are busy observing it in here and how you are coming across. That's on your mind.

Dean: It might be. I can't readily say I accept that it's totally true, but I have found also, just almost a whole hour I thought about being sad, I readily accept that. Maybe a week from now I may say what you said is true. I don't know.

Zois: You are much more in touch with the sadness?

Dean: Yes. I would like to get rid of it. I really would.

Zois: We see in the past the anger and the sadness would immediately generate anxiety and cause the muscle spasms.

Dean: If that's what it is. I'm not sure that I accept that.

Zois: Were there ever any other physical problems?

Dean: I was told I have a torn rotator cuff. I have a couple of discs that are, those things are really okay. But I'm beginning to believe that, real or not, the pain levels that come with them are surely in my head, governed by my head much more than the reality of the problem. I believe that. I accept that.

Zois: How have things been going for you over the past month?

Dean: The business has improved tremendously. My relationship with Kim just swings like a pendulum. I am making a conscious effort not to lock her out. Our agreement is that she can ask me anything she wants and if I'm comfortable discussing it with her I will. If I'm not then I won't and she won't bug me about it. I think for the moment that is a fair way to handle it.

Zois: How do you compare it with in here?

Dean: I try in here to answer everything, but sometimes we both know that anger just rears up. Right now, something that you said or my reaction to it, I just got a pain in my ass.

Zois: When I speak about in here, between the two of us, you have a reaction to that?

Dean: Yeah, I had such a terrible rectal pain. I can feel my sphincter in spasm. Is that the anger?

Zois: Just now when I referred to the two of us—

Dean: It must be the anger.

Zois: —you became very anxious.

Dean: I am not aware that I became anxious other than I felt that sudden pain. If you are saying to me that the tremendous increase in pain level or the bringing it on in a period where it's fairly comfortable is a sign of anxiety, I'll accept it. I had never thought of it that way.

Zois: You have reported here over these sessions, that you have been very anxious in this room.

Dean: Terribly.

Zois: How do you feel now talking to me?

Dean: Pretty comfortable. But again, am I trusting something that is unreal? If my head says to me that I'm pretty comfortable and then I get one of those zingers, that's my body saying you are not comfortable. Who do I believe?

Zois: As you compare it with the way you felt in those other sessions, how would you compare it?

Dean: Better.

Zois: We saw you were very anxious and defending yourself a great deal in the first sessions.

Dean: Is there the same kind of transference in this analysis as there is in what I've tried before?

Zois: What was it like for you before in the other therapies?

Dean: Nothing.

Zois: What do you mean?

Dean: I never felt anything, but this week you have come into my mind and I realize how angry I am at you and I realize that there is this part of me that is emerging that is so new to accept, new to realizing that it's there and that it works, blames all of these things on you.

Zois: In the other therapy, what were the reactions to those other therapists?

Dean: There were none.

Zois: Would you become angry with them?

Dean: Yeah.

Zois: How would you compare that with the kinds of thoughts you had about me this week?

Dean: I want to scale them. From one to ten, those feelings were down to the two or three level, and I would say these, they vary. I don't think the anger ever goes below seven. I'm not sure if that's a cop-out. I'm not sure if it's easy for me to say to myself, "Blame it on him. It's his fault."

Zois: But that's the emotion you are feeling, whether it's a defense or not, that's the feeling?

Dean: Yes.

Zois: How would you compare the therapy before with this one?

Dean: It was totally wasted. I said to you last week I think I've gotten more understanding in four visits than I did in all of the other years.

Zois: When you have that thought how do you feel towards me?

Dean: It depend's on what's happening. If I'm anxious and my asshole hurts and my legs hurt and I want to cry and I know I'm sad, I'm blaming all of that on you.

Zois: When I asked you the question, "How do you feel towards me when you think about understanding more in four weeks than you did in a prolonged analysis," you went to the times you were blaming me.

Dean: Right.

Zois: But you haven't told me how you feel.

Dean: The sadness and the crying, I want to blame them on you. You make me cry. You make me realize that I'm sad.

Zois: So how do you feel towards me when you think about these things?

Dean: Angry.

I ignore the defensive anger. Again, as with Alan, he wants to use it to divert me.

Zois: What else?

Dean: I think I trust you more today than I have so far. Does that mean, is it two percent improvement or ten percent improvement? I don't know.

Zois: So you say that you trust me more?

Dean: Yeah.

Zois: Generally, are you less anxious and more comfortable in here?

Dean: Yes.

Zois: But you are aware of certain things, you are aware of how you build a wall in here between us.

Dean: Yes.

Zois: And aware that in four weeks things have occurred that haven't occurred in a long time in treatment?

Dean: Yes.

Zois: But you are unable to tell me how you feel about me in that sense. It's easy for you to tell me that you are angry at me.

Dean: No, it's not. It's not easy for me to tell you that.

Zois: But you are in tune with it?

Dean: Yes.

Zois: And you tell me you have certain realizations of what that anger implies to you now?

Dean: Yes.

Zois: But how do you feel towards me as you think about those positive things that have happened?

Dean: I'm afraid of you. I'm afraid that I could really get hooked on you. I don't want to need you.

The craving for closeness with his father gives rise to homosexual anxiety in the transference. This is Session 5 and I elect to make that interpretation later in the treatment. At this point I interpret the anxiety about intimacy.

Zois: So there is that fear of closeness?

Dean: Yeah. I wanted to ask you and I thought about it all week long, if I'm really in trouble is there a way to reach you or don't you believe in that? Do I just have to make it from one week to the next?

The patient introduces abandonment fears.

Zois: So you have the thought that I will be lost to you?

Dean: I want to get up and start walking away. I want an answer to that. I don't know what's good in this process and what's bad in terms of making it work. All I know is that it's working.

Zois: You had the thought that I would not be available.

Dean: Or might not be.

Zois: Have you ever felt that way about anybody else?

Dean: I'm sure.

Zois: Who comes to mind?

Dean: Something that happened with Kim on Sunday. I don't want to be that dependent, I guess, on anyone. Maybe that's one of the reasons that I have the wall.

Zois: There is a lot of fear about being close.

Dean: Yeah.

Zois: What comes to mind?

Dean: Need and dependency. I don't know if they are the right words, but they are the ones that come to mind.

Zois: So what would it be like to lose me?

Dean: To lose you? Both pleasure and pain.

Zois: What comes to mind?

Dean: It would be nice not to come here every week. It would be sure as hell a lot more pleasant not to have to go through the pain.

Zois: You are talking about the pain of coming here, but you are not talking about me. The question is: What would it be like to lose me?

Dean: But you are helping me. That's the other side of it.

Zois: So how do you feel right now as you think about the question?

Dean: It's 50/50.

Zois: What does that mean?

Dean: I can always find somebody else. You are not the only one.

Zois: But that doesn't tell me how you feel about losing me.

Dean: I guess what I'm fighting is I would be sad to lose you. Why does it take so long for me to realize it? Is the defense mechanism so strong that it doesn't want to deal with it, so it can think of nine million different things?

Zois: So the thought of sadness comes to mind?

Persistence in questioning about loss pays off. After I repeat the question a third time the patient admits to sadness.

Dean: Yes.

Zois: How do you experience that sadness?

Dean: Boy, that wall, I can't even get through it.

Zois: What are you experiencing now?

Dean: I want to play football.

Zois: What do you mean?

Dean: That's the thought that came to mind. I had gone out for the varsity football team in high school as a freshman. I was a good runner, a sprinter. I thought I had made the team. They had made the first cut and the second cut and the third cut and the season was just about ready to start. It was the day they were going to give out uniforms, varsity game uniforms, and I really thought I made it. The coach came over to me at the end of practice and I walked to his office at the stadium and he said to me, "I can't carry you. Maybe next year." And that really shook me. I remember I walked back to my locker and I sat down on the bench and I must have gone to get my books and I started to cry. And this big guy, he was the captain sat down and said, "What's the matter?" and I guess I told him and he tried to be nice about it. And I remember there was a hayride that Saturday night and I had a date and had paid. I could cry on you right now. I asked if I could still go and he said, "Sure."

Zois: So you're holding the tears back, *you don't want to allow me to be close to you.* How do you feel right now?

Dean: Shitty.

Zois: What are you experiencing?

Dean: Just so much sadness. I almost feel like I could spend the rest of my life crying. And now I am so pissed off at you, I could kill you right now. I could just walk over there and choke the life out of you.

This is a wonderful illustration of the short-term technique. In four sessions this man is able to acknowledge the pain that he has successfully hidden from everyone in his life. His attempt to defend in the transference through anger is testimony to the overwhelming anxiety of closeness with another man. Again this is generated by his homosexual fears that in turn represent craving for closeness with his father. I once again ignore the anger as an attempt to divert me.

Zois: So you see how difficult it is to show anybody those feelings and to show them to me in here?

Dean: What comes to mind is it's none of your business, but it is.

Zois: You see, on the one hand you feel so sad you could cry the rest of your life, but on the other hand you fight off that sadness all of your life.

Dean: Absolutely.

Zois: And here with me you defend against it, that when you open yourself to me you become enraged.

Dean: Yeah. It's a lot easier to hide behind it than it is to face it.

Zois: So not coming here, would that be like being cut from the team?

Dean: No.

Zois: Losing me would that be like that?

Dean: No.

Zois: How would that be?

Dean: I just immediately say no.

Zois: So how would it be?

Dean: I don't know.

Zois: You say you would be sad?

Dean: It would be sad because the rational part of me says that the best shot I've ever had to straightening my life out is right here, and I would like to try to do it and get it done. But the rage is so strong. I sat here and I said I really would like to kill you right now and I could.

Zois: So you are doing that to isolate yourself. On one hand there is the openness, and on the other hand there is the defensiveness here, and how difficult it is for you to tell me how you feel about me.

Dean: You have to understand, I don't know. That wall must be so high.

Zois: You have the feeling that you would be sad if you didn't come here?

Dean: Something finally came out, but that was something.

Zois: Then the association was the very sad feeling that you had in high school?

Dean: Then it happened during the week, I remember then that it came up.

Zois: At the same time we are talking about feeling sad and losing me.

Dean: You keep saying it and I want to keep rejecting it, so it must be true. I know the thing you want to reject the most, some point down the line, a few days later, I'll come to grips with it and I'll say, wait a minute, they are really true.

We see how the patient struggles to defend against anxiety-provoking material. In spite of that he is making significant progress. He is able to tolerate being in the room with me. In the other therapy he was not able to do this and sabotaged the treatment.

He clearly illustrates the psychodynamics underlying his defensive rage:

1. He cheated his father of a relationship. This generates guilt and lack of entitlement.
2. He craves the closeness he did not have with his father.
3. He has anxiety about closeness and defends against it through rage.

Dean was intractable to treatment in the traditional model. However, he proved to be an excellent candidate for a technique that could get past defenses and expose the underlying pain and sadness. Dean completed treatment in thirty-four sessions. On ten-year follow-up he continued to do well in his personal and professional life.

8

Defenses

THE THREE CATEGORIES: GENERAL, EMOTIONAL, AND INTELLECTUAL

Patients do not rely on one defense; they mobilize several, either alternately or in conjunction with one another. While typically people tend to favor one category of defense over another, attitudes and behavior from all three often interact.

Generalization

The defense of generalization encompasses vagueness, helplessness, nonspecific thoughts and feelings, passivity, and adoption of a victim role. Vagueness is employed to avoid making a commitment to a specific thought or feeling. Patients are using the defense of vagueness when they qualify statements with terms such as : "I think", "I guess," "probably," "I'm not sure," and "sometimes." Generalizations such as "everybody" and "all the time" also function as a form of vagueness.

Passivity and helplessness are ways to avoid taking action or dealing with an issue. Passivity, like other defenses, is a way of masking anger, sadness, and pain. A patient's fear of expressing anger or pain can be so great that taking a passive stance is preferable.

Jamie illustrates how helplessness is used as a defense.

Zois: Are you angry with him?

Jamie: It's just a mixture of feelings, maybe a little bit angry, maybe a little bit hurt, maybe just everything.

Zois: So you are angry?

Jamie: I don't know if—I don't know what I feel.

Zois: Now you become helpless with me. You said you were angry, now you want to buy it back. You say, "I don't know."

Jamie: I don't know what I feel.

Zois: You told me a minute ago you feel angry.

Jamie: You asked me, "Do you feel angry?"

Zois: Now when I ask you about it you want to buy it back. You say, "I don't know what I feel." You become passive with me. Every time I try to penetrate into your life you become passive and vague and try to keep me out.

Jamie: I'm not trying to keep you out. I'm trying to find out what I really feel.

Zois: Can we agree that "I don't know" is a passive and vague statement that tells us nothing?

Jamie: I don't think so. "I don't know" could mean that I don't know.

Zois: You agree a minute ago you said you were angry and now you are reluctant to stay with that. So we see that you have a great deal of difficulty making a commitment. How do you feel right now?

Jamie: Awkward.

Zois: Are you irritated with me when I say these things?

Jamie: No.

Zois: So are you angry with this man?

Jamie: I don't know what I feel.

Zois: Are you angry that he didn't call?

Jamie: No. I mean, I didn't expect him to call.

Zois: So when you say that you were a little angry, what were you referring to?

Jamie: Just the fact that I envy him because he is the kind of person that doesn't really need anybody emotionally.

Zois: Who do you need?

Jamie: I don't know. I seem to be in need of people.

Zois: Who?

Jamie: People who care for me.

Zois: Who cares for you?

Jamie: My husband, the doctor, in a totally different way, but I, I'm not emotionally independent. I'm very dependent and I wish I wasn't.

Zois: Who else have you been dependent on in your life?

Jamie: Nobody.

For the remainder of the session I focused on Jamie's self-sabotage and her attempt to defeat the therapy. To have continued the challenge to the defenses would have resulted in a stand-off, with Jamie's unconscious the only victor.

Working with the intimacy in the transference, "You won't allow me to be useful to you. You want to go to your grave a miserable, unhappy, isolated person," was the way I was able to technically penetrate through her defenses to her emotions.

The Emotional Defenses

The most common emotional defenses are weepiness, depression, and anger. Weepiness is often used to hide anger and sometimes to mask pain or guilt. A patient makes the statement "I was so mad I cried"; this patient uses the defense of weepiness to mask the anger he or she is afraid to show.

A patient who is experiencing intense anger may use depression as a defense. The depression is a defense against the anger and serves as a way of avoiding the underlying issues. Those who have a fear of anger use depression as a defense because it immobilizes them and therefore removes the danger of lashing out. Defensive depression is nonspecific and the mood of the patient is variable.

Anger that derives from internal conflict, a sense of hurt, insecurity, or inadequacy is defensive in nature. It serves as a mechanism for feeling a sense of power and masking a feeling of impotence. Dean is an example of a man who used anger to ward off intense pain and sadness.

The Intellectual Defenses

The third category of defenses is the intellectual defenses. These are cognitive aspects of the psyche utilized to defend against painful emotions. The intellectual defenses allow patients to avoid their emotions by relying on platitudes and excuses to explain their self-defeating behavior.

Rationalization is the most common of the intellectual defenses. Rationalization, besides providing a ready excuse for the patient as to why he or she behaves in a certain manner, also allows for the explanation of others' behavior. A person who uses rationalization when trying to explain the behavior of others is avoiding the emotional reaction he or she experienced. Rationalizations may also be used to explain away other defenses. While rationalizations usually have an element of validity to them, it is important for the therapist to be vigilant in focusing on the defense as it is presented and not on the validity that may be contained within it.

The following patient rationalizes her feelings towards her mother.

Zois: How angry do you become towards her when you think about this?

Joan: I don't know. Do you rate it?

Zois: What comes to your mind when you think about how angry you become with her?

Joan: Well, she just doesn't understand.

Zois: You are rationalizing your anger away.

Joan: There should be no reason why she should want to hurt me. I just think that she's stupid.

Zois: You are rationalizing away your anger.

Joan: Probably.

Zois: What's "probably"?

Joan: I am.

Intellectualization is the retreat to a philosophical stance to avoid the underlying emotions. Unlike rationalization, intellectualization is a nonspecific way of viewing a situation. When patients are intellectualizing they are not referring to themselves or the issue. Instead, they make general comments. This is geared toward inaction. Intellectualization is an impersonal way of dealing with a painful situation. When challenged, patients generally respond with a description, not an emotion.

Here Jamie utilizes the defense of intellectualization.

Zois: How do you feel right now?

Jamie: Life is painful.

Zois: So you intellectualize about life but not how you feel.

Jamie: I would like to talk about one of the topics I mentioned.

Zois: It is difficult for you to tell me about your relationship with your mother.

Jamie: Everyone has a difficult mother. That's life.

Zois: You intellectualize a lot.

Jamie: I do?

Denial is an insidious defense. People who use denial as a defense often isolate their thoughts from their emotions. The denial may be based on ignorance that the feeling exists.

When a patient refuses to answer a question avoidance is being used as a defense. An example of how patients use avoidance when dealing with significant people in their lives is "I was so angry I walked out." That statement does not explain how angry the person was, it describes what he or she did. Avoidance can also take indirect forms, such as sarcasm.

Jamie also demonstrates the defense of avoidance.

Zois: How does that make you feel?

Jamie: I don't know.

Zois: You seem a little tearful. Are you feeling tearful?

Jamie: Just a little.

Zois: Are you holding back the tears?

Jamie: I don't know.

Zois: You say you don't know. You are feeling tearful, but you are not crying. You don't want me to be close to you. You don't want me to see your tears.

Jamie: I don't think so. There are other problems that I wrote down to discuss with you.

Zois: So you want to get off the subject. Is that what you're saying?

Jamie: I don't know if it's really important.

Zois: So you rationalize to avoid solving your problems and therefore stay behind your wall, a beaten woman.

USING DEFENSES TO PREDICT THE LENGTH AND OUTCOME OF A TREATMENT

The types and intensity of defenses are a predictive indicator of how long the therapy is going to take. A symptom neurotic is in touch with feelings and is able to verbalize them. Those with an obsessive character disorder manifest a significant schism between the cognitive and the emotional. If you were to ask a patient, "How do you feel right now?" and the response is "I don't know," that's a predictive issue. The reason for this is that the patient's psyche is a repository of intensely conflicted feelings. The more painful the emotion the more defended the patient. The more defended the patient, the longer the therapy. Passive people, in general, have a great deal of anxiety about their anger because in their minds they are capable of homicidal rage. They constantly avoid confrontation. They are not avoiding confrontation because of their fear of what others will do to them, rather because of the anxiety that they may lose control. You can expect a priori that the heavily defended patient is going to have a great deal of loaded material.

Conversely, the patient who is not heavily defended will not have the kinds of experiences in the past that have given rise to pain, rage, shame, and guilt. This, in simple terms, is the best way to view any patient. This is why the defenses are such an effective barometer of what you can anticipate. Defenses do not exist in a vacuum. A person is not heavily defended for no reason. The reason is always the same: in the face of heavy defenses expect a great deal of intense emotional material. If you think you are getting past the defenses but not getting to the emotions, be careful that the patient is not being compliant. Compliance serves as one way for the patient to avoid digesting the information that the therapy generates. By complying, a patient can avoid experiencing the emotional component of the material. It is impossible that a heavily defended patient has nothing to talk about. When the reverse is true, do not expect to discover very intense material. When the patient is in touch with his or her feelings and is able to verbalize them, that patient's past history with parents, loved ones, and significant others has not been loaded with guilt, rage, homicidal fantasies, and sadism. It is a simple equation: intense defenses equal intense emotions.

HOW DEFENSES NEGATE THE THERAPEUTIC PROCESS

Again, in the face of resistance any exchange of information is valueless. If you are not working within the triangles of person and feeling, you are not conducting therapy. Defenses that negate the therapeutic process do not result in an abrupt failure of therapy. Instead, there is a deterioration of the therapy into an intellectualized process where the therapist interprets, gives advice to, and is supportive of the patient. If you are not successful in getting through the defenses, you will not come to a point in the therapy when the two of you have nothing to say to one another. The reverse is going to happen: you are going to have plenty to say to the patient. Unfortunately none of that is going to be very productive. If you find yourself intellectualizing, the patient is defeating you. From time to time you will find yourself lost at sea. You will be looking for clarification of the dynamic issue and none will be found. You will be looking for the appropriate technical intervention and it will not be readily apparent. The majority of the time, therapist confusion is the result of the patient successfully thwarting efforts to get through. This will have happened over a series of sessions, so you may not be able to identify exactly when it occurred. In order to get back on track you must examine the transference. Just pick up the pace and say to the patient, "How do you feel right now? In your mind what is going on here?" Then ask the patient what he or she thinks the progress of the therapy has been. Then give your opinion and ask the patient how he or she feels about that. Then back to the transference. "How do you feel about me?" or "How do you feel that in my mind you are defeating this process right now?" Therapists frequently feel derailed. This is not because of incompetence or ignorance. It is a transference/countertransference issue wherein the patient has successfully foiled the therapist's attempts to penetrate the defenses. The entire process has become a defense and the therapist is responding to that amorphous defensive posture.

THE NEED TO RESTRUCTURE DEFENSES

Part of getting through the defenses involves an educative process of pointing out what defenses are being utilized.

Doing this repeatedly will lead to a restructuring of those defenses. However, most of the time we find diminution rather than total absence of the defenses. Exhaustion of defenses occurs only through repetition.

THE RESURGENCE OF RESISTANCE

Therapy is a repetitive process. Along with vigilance it takes patience and the ability to repeatedly direct your attention to issues when they arise time and again. The patient does not have the knowledge and background of the therapist. The therapist's tendency to become impatient or bored because of the resurgence of the same defenses is much greater than the patient's. When emotions are tapped into there is the propensity for eliciting defenses repeatedly. The therapist cannot let that go by, nor should the therapist become discouraged. It is part of the process of the therapy. Over time the defenses will diminish and the patient will deal with them in a more appropriate way. Patients develop the ability to recognize defenses on their own. Technically, the resurgence of defenses should be dealt with in a similar fashion to the first time they arose. It is not an opportunity to lecture the patient. The closest the therapist comes to a lecture is the statement, "Do you notice when I make an interpretation you become passive with me as a function of your irritation that I am trying to penetrate into your life?"

9

Emotions

ANGER

Anger is part of the genetic makeup of all human beings. When anger is expressed appropriately, it can lead to constructive behavior. However, anger frequently is colored and distorted by past experiences. An event in the present can trigger memories of a similar event in the past and generate an exaggerated response.

Often people are unaware of the appropriate way to express anger. They equate verbalizing angry thoughts and feelings with acting on them. People who fear their own anger generally do not realize that expressing anger does not mean they have to explode in a fit of rage.

To understand anger in relationships, one must also understand pain and hurt. Patients have many preconceived notions about anger based on experiences of their own and of significant others. Homicidal fantasies are very common. This is the way people indulge their anger internally. However, in the psyche it is a short leap from homicidal fantasy to the belief that anger can be dangerous. Events in the past may have demonstrated the danger of anger. The individual's perception is that anger is negative, no matter what form it takes. The goals of the therapist are first to diminish the patient's anxiety about anger and second to educate the patient that there is an appropriate way to verbalize it. People do not understand that to demonstrate their anger they do not have to lash out verbally or physically. Many patients harbor the belief that anger is negative and the only way to show it is by doing something extreme. Telling someone "I am angry with you" is just as effective, if not more so, than screaming at them. People who scream are those who feel helpless.

This is a 29-year-old male who is recalling an incident with his father. During the evaluation he presented as a passive person who spoke in a low monotone. In the following vignette he reveals the etiology of his emotional paralysis.

Zois: It's similar to your father?

Gerard: Yeah.

Zois: He would press you?

Gerard: Sure.

Zois: How would you feel with him?

Gerard: I would be angry about it.

Zois: How angry would you be with him?

Gerard: Very angry with him.

Zois: How angry would that be? What would you see in your mind?

Gerard: One time I was so angry I chased him with an axe, but I wouldn't have hit him with it. I was just angry.

Zois: You have the thought of hitting him. You are very anxious as you think about it.

Here again I take the denial and turn it around.

Gerard: Yeah. It was terrible.

Zois: What had happened?

Gerard: It was just that all the frustrations had built up about our work and what we were doing.

Zois: What happened that particular time? What did he do?

Gerard: That's what I felt so bad about. That one instance wasn't so important.

Zois: What was it?

Gerard: I never actually envisioned hurting him or anything like that. As a matter of fact when I picked it up and realized, I just threw it down and was just screaming about it.

Zois: He said something to you? Is that it?

Gerard: Well, no. We were doing construction for the house and he was always taking shortcuts and I felt if we were going to do something we should do it right and he was always pressuring me to get it done.

Zois: What happened that time?

Gerard: On this particular instance we didn't have enough cement and he wanted to do it. He wanted to do it even though we didn't have enough cement and he wasn't making the mix right. I said, "Look, let's wait until we get more cement and let's do it right." It was a build-up of that, a lot of things happened that day.

Zois: Where were the two of you standing?

Gerard: On the foundation that we were building.

Zois: Where was the axe?

I ask for details to place the patient in the scene. This will facilitate his experiencing those emotions in the room.

Gerard: It was next to me.

Zois: Did you say something to him first?

Gerard: I said, "You make me so mad." And I picked it up and I threw it down on the log.

Zois: What was his reaction?

Gerard: He was in shock.

Zois: You say you chased him with it?

Gerard: I ran two steps with it then I threw it down. I didn't really chase him with it.

Zois: What did he do when you did that?

Gerard: It took him aback. He must have been really upset about it.

Zois: What did he say?

Gerard: Nothing.

Zois: As you think of it now what do you picture if you had struck him?

Gerard: It would be awful.

Zois: What do you see in your mind?

Gerard: He would be seriously hurt.

Zois: Where would you strike him? Remember this is your fantasy.

I interject this to allay the patient's increasing anxiety at the thought of killing his father.

Gerard: In the head.

Zois: Where in the head?

Gerard: On top I guess.

Zois: You say you guess. It's your fantasy.

Gerard: On top.

Zois: What would he look like?

Gerard: He'd be covered with blood.

Zois: How do you feel as you think of that?

Gerard: It's terrible that I have to get that angry [he bursts into tears].

Zois: You are tearful.

Gerard: Yeah.

Zois: You have mixed feelings about your father?

Gerard: Um-hmm.

Gerard had it all with his father: anger, guilt, sadness. Each issue had to be clarified and interpreted. The breakthrough came in the above sequence when I desensitized him toward his rage and helped him experience his conflicted feelings. This is a good illustration of the need to ask for details in order to enable the patient to relive that moment in the transference.

PAIN

Gerard came to treatment suffering intense sadness. One of the goals of his therapy was to emerge from the process capable of verbalizing his pain. That ability was colored by a misconception he harbored: to admit being hurt is to admit weakness. It is appropriate to make the interpretation of the fear of being vulnerable to the patient in the transference: "So you don't want to risk your neck here with me." As with anger, there is an educative component to the process. Gerard's depression abated after completing the work on the above issues. Many of the transferential issues related to his father.

Jamie's therapy dealt with similar issues in relation to her mother. Here she is discussing the pain associated with feeling abandoned by her mother.

Zois: When did you come to this country?

Jamie: When I was 14.

Zois: What was the reason for coming?

Jamie: I went to school. More than that was that my mother was, well if anyone had money, it's sort of a way of showing it, to send your child away. So she sent me away.

Zois: So your mother sent you away?

Jamie: Yeah.

Zois: How do you feel about that?

Jamie: I would never do it to my child.

Zois: How do you feel about that?

Jamie: It was a good experience because—

Zois: Do you notice you didn't answer my question? How do you feel that your mother sent you away?

Jamie: I don't feel anything.

Zois: You say, "I would never do it to my child."

Jamie: Because it was a very lonely experience.

Zois: How do you feel about your mother making you lonely?

Jamie: I don't know. You're asking me all of these questions [tearful].

Zois: You appear upset. How do you feel about me asking you all of these questions?

Jamie: I don't know.

Zois: You are crying. You are having a reaction. What's the feeling?

Jamie: I don't know. You always ask what it is I feel. I don't know.

Zois: What do you feel?

Jamie: Obviously upset.

Zois: You are crying.

Jamie: She didn't love me. I'm crying because of the things she did to me.

It was difficult for Jamie to acknowledge her sadness at the thought that her mother did not love her. The issues of victimization, guilt, anger, and sadness were subsequently explored. She was able to place her relationship with her mother in perspective after she was able to recall happier experiences.

GRIEF AND SADNESS

There is an appropriate mourning period when faced with loss. The problem occurs when the experience of the grief and sadness becomes extended or even lifelong. Pathological mourning is evident when an individual cannot speak about a deceased person without tears. The goal of the discussion of every relationship is to be able to view it in an appropriate, balanced way. All relationships contain positive and negative feelings. It is appropriate to recall someone who has died with sadness. Just as important is the appreciation of carrying with you in memory the elements of the relationship that have enriched you. The therapist must understand these elements if the therapy is to have a successful conclusion. Life is about relationships, therefore life is about loss. The ability to tolerate loss is one of the cornerstones of mental health.

Hal is recalling the death of his father.

Zois: When did your father die?

Hal: In 1963.

Zois: What did he die from?

Hal: Lung cancer.

Zois: When was the last time you saw him alive?

Hal: Seven days before he died.

Zois: Where was that?

Hal: In the hospital.

Zois: What did he say to you?

Hal: He was unable to say anything.

Zois: What did he look like?

Hal: Terrible, terrible.

Zois: In what way?

Hal: He was discolored. I was told that he had banged his head or something at one point. He had tubes in him. He had an expression of pain on his face. Most of the time his eyes were closed.

Zois: Was he aware that you were there?

Hal: I couldn't be certain.

Zois: When was the last time you actually spoke to him?

Hal: It was before he went to the hospital and told me that he was scheduled to go to the hospital, that he hadn't been feeling very good, that he was going there for tests. I don't think he knew at the time that he was going to have an exploratory operation.

Zois: Did you know?

Hal: No.

Zois: Did he tell you this in person or on the phone?

Hal: In person.

Zois: What did he look like?

Hal: He was thinner than usual and withdrawn and obviously depressed.

Zois: You say seven days before he died you saw him in the hospital?

Hal: Yes.

Zois: What happened in the intervening seven days?

Hal: I went to see him in the hospital in Connecticut. I was living in Virginia and so I went back home, having heard from my sister and his physician that they didn't think he was going to last more than a week.

Zois: When were you told that?

Hal: In the hospital.

Zois: Then you went back to Virginia?

Hal: Right.

Zois: So the last time you saw him was there, and you were told he was going to die?

Hal: Yes.

Zois: What did you say to your father before you left his bedside?

Hal: I took him by the hand and said—I don't know what I said.

Zois: You are becoming vague again.

Hal: Yeah.

Zois: What did you say to your dad?

Hal: "You're going to be all right."

Zois: Did you say anything else to him?

Hal: "It's me. I'm here." I was angry with him that he didn't talk to me, because he opened his eyes a couple of times. I said, "Dad, it's me. It's Hal. Here I am. How are you feeling? What's happening?" And I couldn't get a response from him. And I had a feeling he was angry at me.

Zois: You had this feeling?

Hal: Yes.

Zois: In your mind what would he be angry about?

Hal: That he was just so disappointed in me that I didn't fulfill what he wanted in a son.

Zois: In the hospital as you took his hand, you had this thought?

Hal: Yeah.

Zois: How do you feel at this point as you think about that?

Hal: He was dying and disappointed and angry.

Zois: How do you feel now as you think about it?

Hal: It was sad and awful.

Zois: How do you feel right now?

Hal: Sad.

Zois: Did you declare your feelings to him?

Hal: No.

Zois: You never said good-bye to him?

Hal: No. I never said, "Dad, I love you and I just want you to know that."

Zois: Have you had thoughts about that since that time?

Hal: No.

Zois: Is this the first time you have thought about it?

Hal: First time I ever said that, "Dad, I love you and I want you to know that."

Zois: How do you feel as you say those words?

Hal: Sad.

Zois: How do you experience that sadness?

Hal: It's a heaviness in my body.

Zois: It is painful for you to think that you put your father in his coffin and you didn't say this last good-bye?

Hal: Yes [tearful].

Zois: So you punish yourself that in your mind you were not a good son.

GUILT

Hal demonstrates that one of the most intense emotions is the guilt elicited towards someone who has died before that relationship was appreciated in its total complexity. The most curative approach to guilt is to help the patient understand that they indeed may have done something wrong, in the same way that no relationship is without positive and negative feelings. This poses an important issue because it is easy enough to deal with a patient who feels neurotically guilty, but there are times when the person is justified in experiencing guilt. We all, at times, behave in a way that we regret. There is a larger question that has been asked of me by many patients: "What if I really did do wrong?" What can the therapist say in response? Supportive statements constitute a frivolous approach. The impulse of the therapist too often is to jump in and attempt to convince the patient that they have no reason to be guilty. One of the most common kinds of vignettes is "My father died and I wasn't at his bedside." To attempt to convince the patient that he should not feel guilt is not the approach here. What is necessary, because guilt is a fact of existence, is the ability to acknowledge that we do wrong at times. The task of the therapist is much easier when the patient's guilt is exaggerated, unfounded, and unjustified, but the larger issue is when someone says I did wrong and the rationalizations and the excuses are gone. The patient has to confront that issue and the emotions that exist.

Therapists do not want to see people suffer and we do not want to believe that they are capable of certain terrible actions. There is a countertransference issue when patients do wrong. You do not want to believe that they are capable of behaving in certain ways. You certainly do not want to believe that you are capable of that. The therapist has to help the patient live with it. That is the goal. Guilt is a very complex concept because it leads directly into "What do I do if I have done wrong?" This is a philosophical as well as psychological issue. Here the advice to the therapist is: do not try to dodge that issue, certainly not for countertransferential reasons. In the end, the same way we live with the memory of someone who has passed on and feel enriched and have to keep the negative in perspective, the patient and therapist have to live with justified guilt. It is the acknowledgment of those issues and the understanding that we have to live with them that hopefully molds our present and future behavior. That is more therapeutic than any supportive statements.

Hal continues to discuss his brother and the guilt associated with his death.

Zois: Have you always been aware of how tightly you held on to your feelings and bottled them up and isolated yourself?

Hal: Yes. The same is true when my brother died.

Zois: How old were you then?

Hal: Eleven. When the family gathered at the house after the funeral my uncle said to me, "He's better off." My brother spent almost his whole life in an institution.

Zois: How did you feel when your uncle said that, "He's better off"?

Hal: I don't remember.

Zois: How do you feel now when you think about that?

Hal: I associate it with myself.

Zois: How do you feel right now?

Hal: Sad and angry combined.

Zois: You associate it with yourself in what way?

Hal: That I can substitute myself for my brother. My uncle saying, "He's better off."

Zois: You've had that thought?

Hal: Yes.

Zois: Did you ever put yourself in your uncle's place and have the thought that your brother would be better off dead?

Hal: Yes, I had death wishes for my brother. I wished he were dead.

Zois: What would those wishes be like?

Hal: That he would die. That he would get into some kind of conflict and that he would die, he would be killed.

Zois: You had the thought that he would be killed in a fight. How would it happen?

Hal: There were these fights that broke out there and we were aware of them when we would go to see him sometimes.

Zois: How were you aware of them?

Hal: He looked as if he were in a fight.

Zois: How would you know?

Hal: Black eye, bruised along his face, and he would complain that he had been in a fight.

Zois: How would you picture him being beaten to death, with what?

Hal: Some object, a chair, a broom with a post, something that somebody would beat on his head.

Zois: What would he look like?

Hal: Well, he was so horrible-looking to begin with that the whole image of him being beaten down and ending up dead was horror-striking.

Zois: In your mind what would life be like if he were dead, at that time?

Hal: I would be relieved of those awful visits that we made often enough.

Zois: What was awful about them?

Hal: Because I hated him. I couldn't stand his looks and his attempts to pull me close to him. He smelled bad. He looked bad.

Zois: You said he attempted to pull you close?

Hal: Yes.

Zois: How would he do that?

Hal: Like a child hugging a toy bear. He would put me on his lap and my mother would tell me not to be afraid.

Zois: He was affectionate towards you?

Hal: Yes.

Zois: When he would see you what was he like?

Hal: He was happy to see me.

Zois: He would want to hug you and hold you?

Hal: Yes.

Zois: How do you feel about him now as you think about him reaching out to you and trying to be close to you?

Hal: It was just a sad thing and—I couldn't take it. I just couldn't take it.

Zois: On your side, he was somebody who cared about you?

Hal: Yes.

Zois: How do you feel as you think about that?

Hal: I felt I couldn't give myself to him.

Zois: How do you feel right now as you think about this?

Hal: It's an intensely sad situation.

Zois: How sad is it for you?

Hal: Very.

Zois: How do you experience that sadness?

Hal: I feel a heaviness in my chest.

Gerald, Jamie, and Hal illustrate the interrelationship among anger, sadness, and guilt. The legacy of this trinity of emotions is self-sabotage and lack of entitlement. Hal's emotional paralysis was more intense than Jamie's or Gerard's because he had to deal with the pain and guilt in relation to his father and his brother. His childhood and adult life were permeated with sadness. He achieved relief when he was able to resolve the conflict underlying those relationships.

10

Midphase of Therapy

THE SESSION

The patient is a 35-year-old female, married, with three children. She entered treatment because she was depressed, had passive suicidal ideation, a poor relationship with her husband, and suffered with fantasies of murdering her youngest child, a four-year-old daughter. This fantasy caused her much pain and upset. The fantasy remitted after a two hour evaluation in which she came to realize that it was her way of punishing herself for intense guilt. The session below is Session 9. The patient has discussed her conflicted relationship with her father and her meager relationship with her mother in earlier sessions. The patient comes in and is upset that she did not have an extra session last week. She felt she was getting to relevant material and was not able to schedule because of my time constraints. She now comes in registering her upset.

In the process of clarifying and challenging the defenses, I work with the transference.

LACK OF ENTITLEMENT

Caroline: I feel like I want to leave that behind, you know, leave him behind. I think about that and I feel upset. One thing I thought of was the feeling that as bad or as harmful or whatever as it may be, at least that's the way things have been. That's the way I am comfortable with things. So to change things, it's hard to think about.

That is a rationalization, but I do not make that interpretation. Instead I say:

Zois: So there is a thought that you are not entitled to more?

I choose to deal with her lack of entitlement.

Caroline: Well, it's not exactly not entitled. It's just being afraid of the unknown.

Zois: What does that mean? It's a rationalization.

GUILT

Now I point out the defense—the rationalization—and what engenders the defense is the lack of entitlement, the guilt. I am working with two issues with the patient. She again responds with a defense.

SELF-SABOTAGE

Caroline: What's that?

Zois: You say things have been bad and continue to be bad for you?

Caroline: Well, not that they should be, but that's what I'm used to. It's hard for me to change.

Zois: Isn't that a rationalization to keep you the way you are, to keep punishing yourself?

I am touching on the defense and I am touching on the underlying guilt. Then she uses another defense: she becomes general.

Caroline: Maybe. I don't know.

Zois: Well, what do you call it?

I challenge, clarify, and interpret the underlying guilt through self-punishment.

Caroline: That's just the way it is. That's just the way I feel.

Zois: But this thought that that's the way it is, that is a rationalization. What you are telling me is that you are full of conflicts about your father and that you don't deserve to let go.

Caroline: Well, I don't look at it in those terms. It's just that I can't for whatever reason.

Zois: Well, "I can't for whatever reason" is a vague and passive comment.

Caroline: Yes. Well, I'm saying I don't understand what the reason is.

Zois: Which is more passive. Yet you report that you had the thought that your father died nine years ago and the tears came to your eyes. Can we look at that?

Caroline: We can try.

Zois: What is that telling me? We can't go on from here?

The patient uses the defense of helplessness: "We can try." I interpret, and she continues in the same vein.

Caroline: No.

Zois: Well?

Caroline: It's just that I don't know.

Zois: What are you telling me?

Caroline: Just that. I mean—

Zois: So there is still a part of you that doesn't want to look at it, wants to go on, as you say, the old way, feeling the pain, wishing yourself dead, punishing yourself with various thoughts?

Caroline: Yes.

Zois: And doing things to punish yourself.

Caroline: Yes.

Zois: So, "We can try" is a way of saying "I want to continue that way."

Caroline: Well, it's not that I want to.

Zois: Who is being passive?

Caroline: Well, I am, but—

Zois: That passivity is a function of your wanting to keep the old way.

Caroline: Yes.

Zois: So if it's not you, then who is it?

Caroline: I didn't say that it wasn't me. I just feel like I've never had much success in looking at that.

Zois: So then you should continue to fail?

Caroline: No.

Zois: You should continue in the old way and you should continue the old way in therapy?

Caroline: No, I don't want to, but. . . .

Zois: But there is always the "but."

Caroline: Yes.

Zois: So? Who is in charge of your life?

Caroline: I feel like I am.

Zois: So who is carrying the suitcases? You smile.

Caroline: Well, I am now, but I don't know what to do with them. I want to get rid of them.

Zois: So you are passive with that?

We see continuous challenging and interpreting. The patient has no problem throwing up one defense after another—rationalization, helplessness, vagueness—in an attempt to keep me away from the feelings.

Caroline: Yes.

Zois: So on one hand you report that you were almost there. Now you say you don't know what to do with them?

Caroline: Yeah, but that was a week ago.

Zois: This is what, ancient history now?

VICTIMIZATION

Caroline: Yeah. That's how I feel as far as my access to it.

Zois: Now you are buried. I've deprived you of it and it's not here now. Hmm?

Caroline: Yeah.

Zois: So it's either I'm to blame and then when I'm asking you, then you tell me that you can't. So on the one hand your father deprived you of a relationship. I deprive you of freedom from that conflict. Hmm? So where are you in all of this?

I work in the triangles of conflict. I bring in her father, and touch on her sense of victimization and how she uses being victimized as a defense: she could not have her session two days in a row.

Caroline: Sitting here waiting to be told what to do.

Zois: Well, where is that going to get you?

Caroline: Obviously, not much of anywhere.

Zois: You are telling me you don't want to get anywhere. There is a part of you that wants to suffer.

Caroline: That's only part of me.

Zois: So where is the other part?

Caroline: I don't know.

Zois: What?

Caroline: I don't know.

Zois: Passive?

Caroline: Obviously someplace.

Zois: Someplace? Does that help us?

Caroline: No, but I don't know what will.

Zois: So I'm useless. Your husband is useless. Your father is useless.

I make the interpretation of three components of the triangle.

Caroline: Yes, yes, because I'm the one that has to do it.

Zois: You tell me.

Caroline: And I can't.

Zois: And you can't. So this is another failure for you, you tell me. Is that it?

Caroline: That's how it feels sometimes.

Zois: Well, are you failing today to get back at me for not having the extra session?

Through the transference I interpret her need to satisfy two impulses: one, to get back at the significant people in her life who she feels have victimized her, and two, to fail and to use me as the excuse. I make the interpretation, "Are you failing here to get back at me for not having the extra session?" This is one of the key interpretations in the transference.

Caroline: Am I failing what?

Zois: Are you failing here today in order to get back at me for not having another session?

This patient has a habit, which I do not challenge at this point (but I could), that when I make an interpretation that is close to home, she repeats the question, she becomes obtuse, which is another mode of defense. "Am I failing what?" I was very clear and she knows it.

Caroline: No, that's not going to help me.

OEDIPAL TRIANGLES

Zois: But that reality doesn't help the way you feel. Is that what you are doing? Are you trying to fail at life to get back at your father?

Caroline: No, I'm not trying to fail. It's just the way it is.

Zois: So you are failing in life to get back at him?

Caroline: No. He doesn't care. He didn't care then, he wouldn't care now if he were here.

Zois: So you are failing and you're banging your head against a brick wall for this man who in your mind was uncaring, but you try anyway.

Caroline: Yeah. I don't know. I just feel so helpless to put all of that aside. It just seems like it should be easy enough to do.

Zois: How was it when you thought about your father dying?

I move to the emotions surrounding her father's death to avoid an impasse.

Caroline: I try not to think about it.

Zois: But you say you did think about it.

Caroline: No. I had really mixed feelings about it. Part of me said that it didn't matter. I said that it was easier that he is gone, because I don't have to deal with him anymore. At least I tell myself that, but obviously I do. That's how I want to feel; that he's gone and that it doesn't matter anymore. It just seems so hard to accept things the way they are.

I'm thinking about the fact that coming here for however long it is and supposedly things are supposed to be getting to the point where they are better and in some ways I feel like nothing has changed that much.

Clinically things have improved with the patient. Her depression is less severe. However, when I attempt to get between her and her father, she musters all the defenses, and now wants to provoke me by saying she is not really any better. Even in the light of the progress she has made this far into the therapy, she refuses to give up the father. And then she says it:

Zois: In what ways?

Caroline: Just that all of that stuff from my father is hanging over me still, and that I haven't let it go.

Zois: So he's very much in your life?

Caroline: Yeah.

Zois: On the one hand you say he was aloof and uncaring. On the other hand there is this intense relationship.

Caroline: It was intense in a negative sense, yeah. I was thinking last night about making decisions and why it's so hard and just realized that I always felt like I have to figure everything out as far in the future for everything I can see, for all of the consequences and I have to make the right decision, because if I have it wrong, it's just going to be awful. It's like I'm going to get yelled at for making the wrong decision.

Zois: Who is going to yell?

Caroline: My father, but he's not here to yell. I mean, that's the feeling.

Zois: So it's your father again?

Caroline: No.

Zois: Who is the man in your life?

Caroline: It's the influences here.

Zois: So when I say it's the man in your life you say that it's the influences here, but *your relationship with him prevented you from allowing any other man to take his place.*

This interpretation has consequences for the unhappy components of her marriage. It also has transference implications, because I also am trying to get between her and her father. I continue to talk about her father. What I am trying to do here is to bring into focus the conflict within the relationship. She, in order to ignore and minimize the deep attachment she has, has attempted in her mind to dismiss him as an uncaring man. It is important in therapy to achieve a balanced view of the individual. However, if she is going to have that relationship come into perspective, she has to acknowledge the intense feelings she had toward him.

If a patient comes in and says, "My relationship with my father is not important; he never cared about me, I didn't care about him," it is a mistake to accept that at face value. If anything, it indicates that there is an intense relationship. The defense against the intensity of the impulses in that relationship is to dismiss the parent as uncaring.

The goal is to elicit an acknowledgment of those intense feelings. By doing that, a balance is brought forth between her father as totally uncaring and her father in an intense relationship with her. She will then be poised to begin to see him as a person, and as someone whom she did care about. To have her acknowledge that those feelings were hers, and that she was not victimized, is paramount.

Caroline: It doesn't make any sense. I mean, it does. Why do I have to do that? I don't know how to make that different. I feel like there must be something that I'm not doing or not seeing or not—something I'm doing wrong [tearful].

Zois: What were your thoughts about your father the other day?

Caroline: What do you mean?

Zois: Well, you said you thought about him when you were coming here. What were your thoughts on that?

Caroline: That it ought to be significant, but that I didn't feel it was.

Zois: So where do the tears come from?

Caroline: Well, I tell myself that I don't care that he's gone.

Zois: So where do the tears come from?

Caroline: I don't know. I shouldn't feel that way. I don't know where they come from. I feel guilty about feeling that way. See, I just don't want to have anything to do with him. I want to just forget that he was ever there.

Zois: So on the one hand you say that, but on the other hand we see that you have a lot to do with it.

Caroline: Yeah, he was there. That's the problem.

Zois: But you were there also. And that's what you deny, that you actively filled in for your mother in an attempt to get him to recognize you, and you rationalized it by saying that you were keeping the peace.

Caroline: I was trying to win his approval by trying to keep the peace.

Zois: Were you winning his approval by keeping the peace or by taking your mother's place?

Caroline: I was thinking about the time when she told me about sitting there with the gun and thinking—it just really surprised me when she told me, and I knew somewhere in my mind that she was thinking about suicide, not about murder. But it's like I was still so shocked when she told me that, because I just sort of assumed that she would kill him right off. When she told me she was thinking of killing herself, at first I was shocked, then I was really angry that she was going to leave us with him. Maybe I'm not conscious of any thoughts about that.

Zois: So she was basically absent in the house?

Caroline: Absent.

Zois: She didn't do much?

Caroline: That's true.

Zois: So you didn't have to get rid of her. She was gone already.

Caroline: Right. She didn't do a lot of things he expected her to do.

Zois: So in personality was Mark closer to your father or your mother?

Caroline: I guess it would have to be my mother.

Zois: You say "I guess."

Caroline: It was my mother.

Here again I make an interpretation that has to do with her guilt, that she displaced her mother. Much of this material has to do with her belief that she was not entitled to be a mother. The self-punishing fantasies of murdering her child were engendered because the painful guilt, sadness, and rage was in both relationships, with her father and her mother.

Caroline: But I didn't take my mother's place.

Zois: How do you feel about that?

Caroline: I don't know. I just had a flash or feeling of relief that I wasn't her, but I feel like I wish I were her because he did love her, obviously.

Here the patient comes to an awareness of unconscious material. What emerges is that she wishes she were her mother because she wanted her father's love that much.

Zois: So if you were her, then he would love you?

Caroline: Yes. Except sometimes it didn't seem like he loved her, either. I don't know how he could have treated her the way he did if he loved her.

Zois: That's not the issue.

Caroline: That's the way he treated us too.

Zois: So he treated you—

Caroline: He didn't love us either.

Zois: He treated you the way he treated your mother?

Caroline: Yeah.

Zois: So then what was the difference between you and her?

Caroline: She was there first.

Zois: And if you had gotten there first?

Caroline: I don't know.

Zois: What?

Caroline: I don't know, I just—

Zois: Why, you just had a reaction to that. What came to your mind that you reacted?

Caroline: The idea was that it's a ridiculous question.

Zois: Did you ever think of this?

Caroline: I wasn't there first.

Zois: Did you ever think about that?

Caroline: Not that I remember.

Zois: Because you said "She got there first." So who got there first was on your mind.

Caroline: I know.

Zois: What?

Caroline: I must have thought it or I wouldn't have said it.

Zois: Did you ever think of her as out of the picture?

Caroline: No. Not that I remember, anyway.

Zois: So in that sense, you were accepting of your lot in life as you are now when you talk about having the burden, that she got there first and that was it. So you are still living that?

Caroline: Yes.

Zois: Doing fill-in?

Caroline: Yeah.

I touch on the issue that she is not able to give up her father and accept her husband and children as the primary people in her life.

Zois: You say to me that there is a part of you that wants to continue that fill-in role with your father and at the same time you have your own husband and your own children. There is a part of you that is still doing the fill-in work. Hmm?

Caroline: Yeah.

Zois: And that you feel powerless to stop that in your mind and go on.

Caroline: Yeah, I can't say that I'm not going to do that anymore. It's sort of pointless, now. I feel like I'm back to square one. I feel like I've been over the same thing, over and over and over again and it doesn't change anything.

Zois: So when we examine these issues, you inform me that it's not going to do any good.

Caroline: I don't—no, I'm just saying that it doesn't seem like it has. It's still there. We keep talking about the same thing over and over and over again.

Zois: So you are not going to give up the old way?

Again I move to the defense, and she goes back to the helpless position. But I stay with it.

Caroline: It's not a question of not doing it, it's a question of not being able to.

Zois: What stops you?

Caroline: I don't know.

Zois: So you're helpless to change things.

Caroline: Because if I knew what it was, maybe I could face it and say, okay, that's—

Zois: We keep going around the issue here.

Caroline: Yeah, I know. That's what I'm saying.

Then I make the interpretation about the guilt and the lack of entitlement.

Zois: But you are determined to convince yourself that there is no hope for you, that in the end I will be defeated in my attempts and that you will leave here with all of that baggage.

Caroline: Yeah.

Zois: And you will perpetuate the way it's been.

Caroline: Yeah, because I'm the one who has to do it. You can't do it.

Next I say something that a therapist should always say to a patient in this circumstance:

Zois: So with my failure, I can afford to fail. I'll say that I did—

Caroline: Yeah, you did your best.

Zois: I'll say that I did my best and I'll say—

Caroline: That I didn't cooperate.

She's filling in the blanks for me.

Zois: And you will go on carrying your baggage around. So why do you want to do that to yourself?

This last question is the appeal to the unconscious.

PASSIVITY IN THE TRANSFERENCE

Caroline: I don't. This is what I'm used to doing.

Zois: You see, when I try to get to this issue, you become irritated with me and you become passive.

She demonstrates her passivity by asking me another passive question. We see here the appeal to the unconscious, the interpretation of the helplessness, and the challenge to the passivity and the victim role.

Caroline: How do I become passive?

Zois: You rationalize it: "I'm used to doing this," "That's the way it is," "I don't know how to do it any different." Those are all rationalizations.

Caroline: I know they are. What do you want me to do differently?

I do not take the bait and attempt to answer her question. Instead I move to the transference.

Zois: How do you feel right now?

Caroline: Very frustrated.

Zois: How do you feel toward me?

Caroline: I feel angry because you seem to know the answer, but you are not going to tell me or you are not going to help me.

Zois: How angry are you?

Caroline: I don't know what to do.

Zois: You express this anger with passivity.

Caroline: Yeah, that's what I do, but I've tried asking you what am I supposed to do and you just tell me that I'm passive when I ask that.

Here the therapist must not yield to the temptation to become supportive, and to instruct the patient as to what to do. That is not going to be therapeutic. If I did not move to the transference I would become bogged down in her defenses. And she would move a step closer to defeating the process.

Zois: So?

Caroline: It seems like it's hopeless.

Zois: The asking itself, is your asking what you are supposed to do conducive to getting out of this bind or does it perpetuate the bind?

Caroline: I don't know. It seems like you know the answer, but you are just not going to tell me.

Zois: So you have the thought that I know the answer?

Caroline: Yeah, you know what I'm supposed to do, but I have to figure it out for myself and you are just going to wait for me to do it.

Zois: So you are saying that I know what to do to free you from your dilemma?

Caroline: You could help me do that.

Zois: Which is it? Either I have the answer and I can free you or not? Which is it in your mind?

Caroline: Well, I feel like you know the answer.

Zois: Now you're retreating from your position.

Caroline: No, I'm just saying, that's how I feel. I feel like you have the answer.

Zois: Now you are saying no?

Caroline: I don't know the answer, so. . . .

Zois: Either I have the answer or I don't.

Caroline: I know that you don't.

I get her to acknowledge that I do not know the answer.

Zois: So why are we talking about it?

Caroline: I'm talking about what I wish were true.

I make an interpretation in the transference.

Zois: A minute ago you are telling me I have the answer and you are angry that I don't give you the answer. So if you know that I don't have the answer, then you are angry at something else and that anger is that I'm trying to get in your life and you are passive to resist me. Did you feel this way about your father, that if he treated you a certain way that you will be all right?

Caroline: I don't think that I ever thought about it that way then, but yeah.

Zois: So is it the same here, that you want to put me in his role the same way in your mind that you put him in that role?

Caroline: He could have—

Zois: "He could have." So you carry around in your mind this image of this man who could make everything right for you. Do you look for that in others?

Caroline: I think I look for that in Mark.

She makes the spontaneous association with her husband. But she says "I think." I challenge:

Zois: You do or you don't?

Caroline: Yeah.

Zois: Can you give me an example of that?

Asking for an example serves two purposes. It forces the patient to support that position, and insures that the patient is not being compliant as another defense.

We are observing a patient who, even though she is defensive, has done much of the work of therapy. Even when she is defensive, she pulls back from it and goes on to give more productive material. This is typical of a patient at this stage of therapy. The defensiveness is now a rear-guard action, I understand this by the expression on her face, her body language, and by the way she is producing. The defenses are easy enough to brush aside, and every time I address them she responds with information. It is an appropriate level of defensiveness at this point in the treatment for someone who is so connected to her father.

She is giving ground by inches. It is trench warfare; however, I am seeing progress. Everything about her has changed so I do not want to be short-sighted or sidetracked into the notion of attempting to convince her that she has improved—which is what she wants me to do. She wants to seduce me into trying to sell her on what is better, so that I will retreat from the important issue, which is that she is still holding on to her father. She knows she is going to have to deal with this. The defenses that are mustered are not major issues.

Caroline: I can't give you any specific example. It's just a feeling that somehow he has to make the decisions and make everything all right. One example I can think of, it's not a specific example, but it's sort of just like you making a decision about things, I mean, just everything in general.

I mean, anything important, Mark will ask me what I think about it. I usually just say, when it comes down to it, "Well, whatever you want to do is all right with me," instead of trying to figure out how I feel about something. I guess it's sort of speaking up about it and whatever. I just let him decide. Then I tell myself that it's not really important because it doesn't matter. I don't have an opinion, so. . . .

Zois: So you want Mark to make everything right?

Caroline: Yes.

Zois: So the only person that it still seems could cut it all is your father. So he's still the champ?

Caroline: It sounds like he's got such power over me, even though I know he doesn't.

Zois: So then what does it sound like?

Caroline: He did have that power. I spent my whole life trying to please him. It didn't do any good. Now I'm telling myself the same thing about Mark, about you, probably even about my kids. I don't know.

Zois: How are things now with your children?

Caroline: Pretty good.

Zois: What's pretty good?

Caroline: Well the youngest is getting into sort of a rebellious stage. It's sort of hard for me. This is just in the last few weeks. It's sort of hard for me to handle, but for the most part I think I do all right. I haven't felt like I'm failing as a mother or anything, which I used to feel. That's one part of my life that has gotten better, so. . . .

Zois: In what way has it gotten better?

Caroline: Well, there I don't feel this need to be perfect with the kids. I don't feel like if I had one little slip that that means the end of the world or that I'm an awful mother or that they're going to be damaged for life or anything like that. I guess I can forgive myself. I can't forgive my father that he wasn't there. He didn't want me to be perfect, that's only what—

Zois: Wanted you to be what?

Caroline: Better.

Zois: Did you try to be perfect—

Caroline: Did I try to be perfect?

Zois: —for him?

Caroline: For him? Yeah. I did.

Zois: How did you do that?

How profitable it is to ask for elaboration. What follows is a description of her passive stance: she got along by getting along. This passivity had to do with the intensity of the impulses she was experiencing. The only way for her to deal with those impulses was to become very quiet and passive and compliant. This is a role she played throughout her life, which finally led to depression.

Caroline: How did I do that? By not making waves, getting good grades in school and always doing what was expected of me, not causing any trouble. It didn't change anything.

Zois: You say, "It didn't change anything."

Caroline: Yeah, talking about having power over my own life. I did everything I could, everything I knew how to do and it didn't—it didn't make things any better. He was just never pleased. He was just never satisfied, no matter what. I didn't—Now I could look at it and see he had—his expectations were too much, but I still feel that I'm the one that failed, instead of that his expectations were impossible.

Zois: How do you feel right now?

Caroline: I don't know. I'm really confused. That's how I am feeling.

Zois: So what's the feeling?

Caroline: I don't know. I'm hurt. I'm angry, but I'm not sure exactly at what.

Zois: You say at what?

Caroline: About what.

Zois: Well, as you look at it.

Caroline: I'm angry that he wasn't perfect and then he expected me to be perfect.

Zois: When you say "perfect," what do you mean by that? What does that mean?

Caroline: What do I mean by that?

Zois: What do you mean by his being perfect? What would that have entailed?

Caroline: Actually, I didn't expect him to be perfect. I just wanted him to love me. That would have—

Zois: That what?

Caroline: That would have been perfect.

Zois: So a part of you still wants to be the victim.

Caroline: I didn't look at it that way. I always thought he had the power.

Session 10

Zois: What were your thoughts about our last session?

Caroline: I felt like I just wanted to cry all week.

Zois: What were your thoughts?

Caroline: I don't know. I had so many of them.

Zois: You are generalizing.

She talks of her sadness about her mother and forgiving her father for not being able to show that he loved them.

Caroline: Well, it was like a train or something. I mean, just one after the other. I was thinking about the idea of taking my mother's place. It sounds so simple or something, but on the surface I would have said she really had it rough. My own conscious thoughts were, when I—if I ever get married, it's going to be someone completely different than my father. There were times when I felt sorry for her. But I hadn't really, I guess I really hadn't let myself think about that whole thing, about how much he must have loved her, even though he maybe didn't show it the way I would think would be the best way to do it. He really didn't love any of us. I never thought in terms of he must have loved her.

Zois: Now what do you think about it?

Caroline: He must have—he stayed. He came back. It's just really hard for me to forgive him, for him not being able to show that he loved us. I know he did. I know that intellectually, but I don't feel it.

Zois: When you say "us," who are you referring to?

Caroline: All of us; me, my mother, my brothers and sisters. It was like he couldn't express that until he knew—until he was dying.

I push for specifics.

Zois: How did he express it then?

THE LETTER

Caroline: Well, he wrote me a letter. I don't know if I ever said anything to the other kids, but he wrote me a letter talking about how he wished he had done things differently and he—about how he never let us know how much we meant to him.

It is significant that she says she does not remember if she ever mentioned that letter to anybody else, which indicated in her mind the exclusivity of the relationship. But she still is struggling with that exclusivity by going from "me" to "us." I pick up on that:

Zois: Did he say "us" or "you"?

The letter was to her and not any of the other siblings. She knows that. We see how slowly and methodically she is surrendering the information. But note—and that is why vigilance in therapy is crucial—she says he was writing the letter to "all of us," yet at the same time contradicts herself and says it was to her. Her unconscious is guiding me. I ask her to be specific, which is technically what I should do. She admits the letter was to her.

Caroline: Well, he said "you." I don't know if he meant me specifically or all of us.

Zois: But—

Caroline: But just for him to say that.

Zois: —you say that you don't know if he wrote to everybody or not?

Caroline: Yeah, I don't know. I mean—

Zois: So you never discussed it with the others?

Caroline: No.

Zois: Did you ever tell them that you received a letter?

Caroline: I don't think so.

Zois: You say you "don't think so."

Caroline: Probably not.

Zois: You say "probably not," but you would remember that, wouldn't you?

Caroline: Yeah.

Zois: So did you tell the others?

Caroline: No.

Zois: You didn't. *What comes to your mind now as you think about that?*

Caroline: What, about the fact that I didn't tell them or the fact that I got the letter? That I didn't tell them? I don't think they would be particularly interested. It didn't mean—

Again the defense of repeating what I am asking her and the rationalization "I don't think they would be particularly interested."

Zois: You want to leave it at that? Is that the answer you want to go with?

Caroline: I mean, I just don't—

Zois: You want to leave it at that?

Caroline: Yeah.

Zois: What?

Caroline: Yeah.

Zois: You smile.

Caroline: Well, I still think they wouldn't be interested. I don't see any reason to tell them. I didn't see any reason then.

Zois: Did you tell your mother that your dad wrote you a letter?

Caroline: I don't think I ever did. I'm sure I didn't then.

First the vagueness, then she corrects herself. Here we see a patient who is producing on her own, with minimal challenging from me.

Zois: So it was between you and him as far as you were concerned? You never told the rest of the family, your brothers or sisters?

Caroline: No, it just never—

Zois: Did you ever ask anyone else if they ever got a letter from him?

Caroline: No.

Zois: So what do you think about that?

Caroline: Well, he had his chance if he wanted to tell them. Whether he did or not—

Zois: You say on the one hand you could never forgive him for not showing all of you that he loved you.

Caroline: Well, I mean, most of it—I didn't mean—

Zois: You say most of it, but in fact when you got a letter, you didn't tell anybody else, nor—

Caroline: No one else was around.

Zois: —nor did you ever inquire as to whether or not anyone else received a letter. So if we look at it, this business of "we" isn't really we at all, is it? When you say, "I never forgave him for not showing that he loved us," you are not talking about us at all, are you?

Caroline: No.

Zois: But that you are trying to deceive yourself and keep a certain truth from yourself by using "us" and "we" and even when you told me about the letter, you substituted everyone for you?

Caroline: Yeah.

Zois: And from others?

Caroline: Yeah. Well, I mean, in the letter he said he wished he had been able to, "show you that I cared about you," but—

Zois: But you changed that.

Caroline: But it was in the context of the family.

Zois: You changed that. You said "all of you"?

Caroline: Yeah.

Zois: Hmm?

Caroline: Well, I could say it could be either you singular or plural.

Zois: You smile and you are not interested whether or not anybody else got a letter?

Caroline: Nobody else was there.

Zois: The fact that you never forgave him for what he did to "all of you" is hypocrisy that you kid yourself with to deny the issue.

Caroline: I said I never forgave him for not loving me.

Zois: A minute ago it was all of you. Now you are looking down and fidgeting with your thumb.

Caroline: I wanted him to love all of us. Maybe we would have been that big happy family.

Zois: Where is all of us? You don't inquire as to anybody else's letter or lack of letter.

Caroline: We didn't talk about that kind of thing.

Zois: You didn't talk about it?

Caroline: We didn't care enough about each other to ask about things like that.

Zois: On the other hand you tell me you are upset about him not caring about all of you, now you say you didn't care about each other. But in fact, it was you and him that you were interested in.

Caroline: Yeah.

Zois: Now you're bluffing about your brothers and sisters.

Caroline: Yeah.

Zois: You have difficulty acknowledging that to yourself. That's the piece that you were getting to the last time when we didn't have that second session, that all of these years, from the time you were filling in for your mother, it was you and him in your mind, right down to when he wrote you the letter and you spent the time denying that to yourself. If you are honest with yourself, isn't that the way it is?

Caroline: Yes.

Zois: Have you ever acknowledged that to yourself?

Caroline: No. I knew that I wanted him to care about me.

Zois: But did you acknowledge that you knew it was an exclusive relationship that you were looking for?

Caroline: No.

Zois: If you're going to be honest with yourself, that's what we're talking about.

Caroline: Yeah.

This is the most significant breakthrough the patient has made about her intense feelings toward her father.

She now confronts herself in terms of the exclusivity she wanted in their relationship. This is dramatically illustrated by her inability to share the letter with anyone else.

Zois: Hmm?

Caroline: Yes. Yes.

Zois: How do you feel right now?

Caroline: I don't know.

Zois: Hum?

Caroline: I don't know. I'm just upset. It's funny. I was going to say that I'm a little bit relieved, but I'm not sure.

Zois: What are your thoughts about that?

Caroline: That it seems to be too easy an answer.

Zois: So what are your thoughts about being relieved?

Caroline: I don't know. It's like I didn't want that to be the answer.

Zois: Can you tell me about that, that you didn't want it to be the answer? Did you ever have a thought that that was the answer?

Caroline: Yeah.

Zois: When was that?

Caroline: I don't know. It was partly after reading this book—the book I read last time—that it occurred to me. That was after the last session, it occurred to me.

Zois: What occurred to you?

Caroline: Well, it just seemed like I was sort of dancing around that whole issue and it occurred to me that I was doing that later.

Zois: When was later?

Caroline: The next day.

Zois: What were your thoughts?

Caroline: That I just didn't want to talk about that because I didn't want that to be true. Partly because I just didn't want to admit that, partly because it just seems too easy. It just seems too obvious. It seems too pat an answer, or something.

Zois: So one time you have a thought that it's a pat answer and on the other hand you say because it was too easy to admit that that was the answer?

Caroline: It wasn't too easy to admit, but it just seems easy enough.

Zois: What was in this book that you made the association with the issue of you and your father and your exclusive relationship?

Caroline: Somehow it seems different now than it was when I thought about it then.

Zois: In what way?

Caroline: I'm not sure. My thought that it was hard to admit that to you, like I could think of it myself and maybe I didn't really even admit it to myself, either. Somehow to admit it to you makes it more real or something.

I move to the transference.

Zois: What about this issue of allowing me to get close to your intimate thoughts?

Having broken through to her impulses toward her father vis-à-vis the discussion of the letter, she now is able to recall a dream.

THE DREAM

Caroline: Well, it's not easy to do. I've spent my whole life avoiding them myself. To try to face them with someone else, that's hard. It's funny, I had a dream, a couple this week, and it seemed so important then, I don't know whether it is now, but I had this dream that I was in—I guess it wasn't here physically, but it was in your office, and I guess it was here because it was someplace I was sort of familiar with, but not real familiar with. But anyway, it was like I was working for you, but I was new on the job or whatever, but it was you. You were sort of mysterious and I hadn't sort of quite figured you out. I don't know what that has to do with the dream, but that was part of the dream. Part of it was that I was new at this. I was new at this job. I wasn't really sure exactly where I was, and I went out to go to lunch. I went out and I was supposed to know my way around sort of, but I really didn't know for sure where I was. I didn't know the name of it very well. So I went out looking for places to go to lunch. I figured there are lots of places to go around here and I went looking around. It just seemed to be all of these real sterile office buildings. I mean, it was not, you know, lively or neighborhoody or whatever, but I finally go to a place where there seemed to be restaurants or whatever. I went in one and it seemed kind of—I knew from the outside that it was a bar or whatever, kind of a bar and restaurant or whatever and I went in. I went sort of back in, there was sort of a bar in front and the back was a restaurant and it turned out it wasn't really a restaurant at all, but it was like sort of like a strip joint or something, or that kind of thing. And I realized that is what it was and I really felt—well, first of all I was really embarrassed, and then I felt really sort of ashamed of myself for not realizing that that's what it was. Right away I wanted to get out of there, but I wanted to sort of be cool about it, like I wasn't really lost or whatever. So I had a hard time getting out or getting up the courage to sort of walk out, I don't know, pretend like I knew where I was all the time, all along.

She makes the interpretation herself.

Caroline: After I woke up, I really—I mean, right away I associated the bar, I related that to my father or the restaurant or whatever to my father. And the whole thing, it was like a lot of different things I associated to. I guess my first thing was feeling kind of lost and not only—but knowing something important was going on, but not knowing what. You know, feeling like I was supposed to know my way around and yet I didn't. And you being there and kind of being mysterious and, you know, the whole idea of working for you and everything, but I didn't really know what it was, what you wanted me to do, that kind of thing.

What I do technically is have her recapitulate the dream. I want the patient to repeat the dream so that she can recall more elements.

Zois: So in the beginning of the dream you were working for me in some place that was my office?

Caroline: Yes.

Zois: What did it look like?

Caroline: I guess kind of like your waiting room out here. Kind of small and sort of empty. Not much personality or something, not much character. Like you would walk in and not be able to tell very much about the person who was there just by looking at it. I mean that just says it. Not being able to tell very much from just walking in. And I felt like I didn't know really what I was doing.

Zois: What did I look like in the dream?

Caroline: It's funny, but I'm not really sure that you were in the dream. I mean, it was you, it was definitely you that was in the dream, but I don't know if you were physically in the dream. If you were, I guess you would just look like you.

Zois: You said in the dream the idea of working for me and not knowing what I wanted.

Caroline: Yeah.

Zois: What are your thoughts?

Caroline: I didn't let myself think about that.

Zois: You mean you had to stop yourself from thinking about it.

Caroline: Yeah.

Zois: So what comes to your mind when you think about that, stopping yourself?

Caroline: I just don't want to have to deal with all of that. I mean, that's—

Zois: So as you look at it now, what comes to mind?

Caroline: What do you mean, what comes to my mind? I just don't want to deal with that. That is what comes to my mind. I want to pretend like that's not there.

Her description of a man in the dream who might be me and not knowing what the man wants from her has oedipal implications.

Zois: So you want to treat that like the relationship with your father. You want to pretend that it's not there, but you see that that got you nowhere.

Caroline: Yes.

Zois: So why do you want to continue on with an approach that we've already seen didn't do very much for you?

Caroline: But that's even more embarrassing than talking about my father.

Zois: So as we look at it then?

Caroline: It's still embarrassing.

Zois: But that doesn't help us that you're embarrassed.

Caroline: No. Well, I mean, part of—it's—I don't—I don't let myself have fantasies.

Zois: You tell me that you were stopping yourself.

Caroline: It's not just you.

Zois: Now you generalize.

Caroline: I don't have fantasies.

Zois: As you look here at me and you, what are your thoughts?

Caroline: That I shouldn't be having those thoughts.

Zois: But we see those thoughts are there.

Caroline: Yes, yes.

Zois: So what are the thoughts?

Caroline: Okay. Having a relationship with you, I guess.

Zois: What does that constitute? What do you see in your mind?

Caroline: Well, the bottom line is that I want you to care about me.

Zois: So what surrounds that?

Now she touches on a common issue.

Caroline: That I've always had trouble in my mind separating those feelings about caring for somebody or somebody caring about me from sex.

Zois: So the tender feelings become mixed with sexual feelings.

Caroline: Yes.

Zois: So what were your thoughts when you were having tender feelings toward me?

Caroline: God. I don't know, just wondering what that would be like to have sex.

Zois: What is the feeling as you think of it?

Caroline: It feels good.

Zois: So, you have tender feelings towards me.

Caroline: Yes. You have been very good to me. Many things in my life are better because of you.

Zois: Now you told me before that in the past when you've had tender feelings toward someone, sexual feelings have come up also?

Caroline: Yes.

Zois: Was it that way with your father?

Caroline: God, not that I was conscious of, no.

Zois: But we see that there is a—

Caroline: That's a pattern, yeah.

Zois: —a parallel here?

Caroline: Yes.

TENDER AND SEXUAL FEELINGS

Zois: Tender feelings you would defend against because of your anxiety about sexual feelings, which would be confused with the tender feelings.

Caroline: Yeah.

Zois: So what we see is that the sexual feelings were really a manifestation of your tender feelings?

Caroline: Yes, like that's the logical conclusion or something.

Zois: So when you would have tender feelings toward someone, there would be this anxiety about being close because of sexual feelings?

Caroline: Yeah.

Zois: So would this happen with your father, that you would keep your distance to defend against any sexual feelings coming up?

Caroline: I don't know. I mean how can I answer that? I wasn't conscious of that, no.

Zois: So then there was that anxiety about that—

Caroline: No. I mean, not that I knew of.

Zois: —as there was here? Now, you say you had to stop yourself when you thought about feeling good about me?

Caroline: Yes.

Zois: And tender feelings toward me, so you never had to stop yourself, nothing ever intruded into your mind?

Caroline: No, no, not like that. No.

Zois: Do you agree that in your life tender feelings have been confused with sexual feelings?

Caroline: Yes.

Zois: How do you feel right now?

Caroline: Is it warm in here or is it just I'm so embarrassed over everything that it's warm?

Zois: Now, in the dream that you had, you said that you then went to this restaurant which became—you became aware that it was really a strip joint. How did you know that in the dream?

Do not accept summary. There is more information to be gotten.

Caroline: Well, the environment, the posters up or advertisements or whatever.

Zois: What did the posters show?

Caroline: It showed strippers or whatever. It was stupid names.

Zois: What kind of names?

Caroline: I don't know. Some silly name. It was just posters.

Zois: There were posters with these women who were strippers?

Caroline: Yeah.

Zois: What did they have on in the poster?

Caroline: I don't know. Not much, I guess.

Zois: So there are these women with very little on?

Caroline: Yeah.

Zois: And they had names of the women?

Caroline: Yeah.

Zois: Which you say were silly names?

Caroline: Yes.

Zois: Do you remember any of them?

Caroline: No. I don't know that there was a name. It was just a poster, advertising.

Zois: So?

Caroline: And the whole place just seemed, it was dark and sort of trying to be respectable, but pretty scuzzy.

Zois: Then you left there?

Caroline: Yeah.

Zois: You woke up and you had the association with your father?

Caroline: Um-hmm.

Zois: What comes to mind?

Caroline: Well, his work room in the basement with all the little Playboy-like pictures in it, for one thing. Plus, I can remember when—I don't know how old I was, it was before we moved, so I had to be 16, 15, somewhere around there, 14. So I was less than that. I can remember he and this other friend of his, they went to a place that had some strippers or whatever. And I can remember him going there a couple of times. I mean, I can remember my mother saying that's where he went.

Zois: So he would go with a friend of his?

Caroline: Yeah.

Zois: And your mother would tell you that he was going to a strip joint?

Caroline: Yeah. I think she told me that. I knew that's where he was going. She must have told me.

Zois: He didn't tell you?

Caroline: No. I guess she figured I was old enough to know.

Zois: How old were you?

Caroline: Like I say, I must have been 13, 14, somewhere in there.

Zois: What was your reaction to being told where he was going, to watch women undress?

Caroline: I don't know. I think I was kind of shocked or—not shocked, but surprised. I don't remember. It was sort of silly, too, in a way.

Zois: You say you were shocked?

Caroline: It seems sort of a dumb thing to do.

Zois: So on the one hand you were shocked and on the other hand you thought it was silly?

Caroline: Well, maybe shocked is a strong word. For one thing, maybe I realized there was such a thing. I had seen ads in the papers. I knew, but I didn't know of anyone that went to anything like that.

Zois: So the idea that your father would go?

Caroline: I thought it was sort of disgusting.

Zois: What was disgusting about it?

Caroline: Well, sort of degrading. I don't know if I thought about it that way then, but that's how I am when I think about the pictures now, and I think about—for one thing, I feel disgusted by it, that it's just really a very degrading thing. It's just sort of disgusting.

Zois: This issue that it's degrading, for you or for who?

Caroline: For the women.

Zois: Is the issue for the women?

Caroline: And for the men too.

Zois: On the one hand it's degrading for the women?

Caroline: Yes.

Zois: What about that?

Caroline: Well, I just don't think I ever understood that.

Zois: To understand what?

Caroline: What that was all about, why that was so intriguing. It was intriguing to me too, but I'm not sure why.

Zois: What was intriguing?

Caroline: Well, the pictures, the magazines, and stuff like that.

Zois: What were you intrigued about?

Caroline: I don't know. Well, obviously something mysterious. I was just curious, I guess.

Zois: When you looked at the magazines what were you intrigued by?

Caroline: I don't know. I didn't know what it was all about. I was trying to figure that out.

Zois: What would be in the magazine?

Caroline: Naked women.

Zois: You were intrigued by these women that were depicted this way?

Caroline: I guess so.

Zois: These were your father's magazines?

Caroline: Yes.

Zois: So you would go into that room and look through his magazines and look at his pictures?

Caroline: Yeah. I had to go looking for them most of the time. I was just intrigued by the whole idea of sex I guess. I guess I probably just got a pretty warped idea of sex or women. Anyway.

Zois: What was that idea?

OEDIPAL FANTASIES

Caroline: Well, sort of being treated like objects, in a way, although I don't ever remember feeling that way, myself, I mean with Mark. Occasionally I have, since we've been having all of these problems, but I don't know. I guess I never saw myself like those women, really. I guess when I was younger I had fantasies about that, because that was the only way I knew, really.

She is saying that she was an object for her father. She reports being intrigued by the magazines that she felt had a meaning for him.

She starts talking about sexual fantasies at this point

that had to do with being the object, being helpless. This is how she felt. This is how she felt she was being treated by her father. Now she is producing material that links her father to intense sexual impulses and fantasies. She goes on to discuss how, in her sexual fantasies, she would be like a stripper. She is able to link these fantasies to her father. Sexual fantasies are important because they frequently are closely related to the core neurotic impulse.

Zois: What were the fantasies about?

Caroline: Well, real masochistic type things, or being the object, being helpless.

Zois: Do you recall specific fantasies in particular?

Caroline: No. I feel like that was the underlying thing to all of it, that somehow women are objects or that's how I was in the fantasies.

Zois: So you would present yourself as a sexual object?

Caroline: Yeah.

Zois: In the fantasy you had been the same thing?

Caroline: Yeah.

Zois: What would you be wearing in these fantasies?

Caroline: I don't know.

Zois: You don't know? *It's your fantasy.* Would it ever be in the role of a stripper?

Caroline: Yeah. I think so, along that type of thing, I guess. I don't remember any specific fantasies.

Zois: You were along the lines of one of those strippers?

Caroline: Yeah. Like the magazines.

Zois: Who would be watching you as you stripped?

Caroline: Hmm? I don't think there was ever a face. It was just sort of a feeling of being on display.

She is a stripper for some faceless person. In the fantasy, she does not want to give that person an identity. She does not want to admit to herself that it is her father.

Zois: Feeling someone watching?

Caroline: Yeah.

Zois: The someone was never identified?

Caroline: No, I don't think so.

Zois: Would you masturbate when you had this fantasy?

Caroline: No.

Zois: Just a thought?

Caroline: Yeah.

Zois: How old were you when you were fantasizing you were a stripper?

Caroline: I can remember that. I was about 14, 15.

Zois: So the fantasy would be you being a stripper and a faceless man would be watching. So you didn't want to know who he was.

Caroline: Yeah.

Zois: Who was it that you knew watched strippers and looked at strippers?

Caroline: My father.

Zois: So the issue is who were you the object for?

Caroline: Yeah. Well, I'm glad you could say it was my father.

Zois: What do you say?

Caroline: Well, I don't know. I guess it was my father. I don't have any specific memories of this.

Zois: You say tender feelings and sexual feelings would become intermingled for you?

Caroline: Yes.

Zois: And that this would fill you with anxiety?

Caroline: Yes.

Zois: When you were growing up in your fantasy you were the stripper for this unknown man.

Caroline: Yeah. I guess I was.

Zois: So for you, as well as for him, there was a lot to the relationship.

Caroline: I don't know. My immediate reaction was to say, no, there was nothing there.

Zois: But in your mind?

Caroline: I guess there was.

Zois: You say "I guess." Let's look at this.

Caroline: Well, there wasn't anything positive. When I think about my relationship with my father, if you ask me about my relationship with my father, how was it, my reaction would be to say, "I didn't have one. There wasn't any."

Again, we see how important it is not to be led astray by definitive statements of denial. They are always stated with great authority: "I didn't have one [relationship with her father] There wasn't any." This statement does not have the same impact as it would have had early in treatment. She uses it now as a defense, not as a belief, because she has made a great deal of progress on this issue.

We can summarize many of the issues that this woman has suffered. From a very early age, she had an intense connection with her father. She claimed that there was no relationship, but the reverse is true. She wants to preserve that connection at all costs.

Like her husband, I, in the transference, become a threat to preserving the integrity of that exclusive relationship. So she will defend against my coming between them. In order for her to accept me and to allow me to be close to her, she has to give up the connection to her father.

By "give up the father" I mean make him the father, the parent who cared about her, whom she cared about, and who had a conflicted relationship with her for a time. To make him a real person rather than the larger-than-life "love object" that no one could replace. The tenacity with which she held on to that view of him undermined all other intimate relationships.

In order for me to be useful to her, I have to enable her to give up her father. On a preconscious level, she understands this, but the impulse to preserve the integrity of that relationship continues, and so she defends against it. She knows that if she establishes intimacy with me it is going to be because she has given up the father.

All the defenses we have seen in the session are in the service of the neurotic impulse not to give up her father.

It is as if there is a little person sitting on her shoulder saying, “Put him aside. Make him a real person. Give up all these impulses and distorted thoughts.” And there is another little person saying, “Don’t do that; he’s all you’ve got. You’ve paid such a great price to hold on to him. You’ve suffered. You’ve been so guilty. You’ve been victimized. You have done everything in the world for him. How can you give him up now?” That is the intrapsychic conflict that I was confronted with from day one, except on day one, there were too many other symptoms: the self-punishing thoughts about murdering her youngest child, the angry thoughts about her husband, the depression, the depletion of psychic energy, viewing the world in dark terms because she was so emotionally drained and depressed. Having worked through those symptoms, we have taken this path.

Now we are at that crossroads where I believe I can make my move, because I have established intimacy with her. She has tender feelings toward me because of the help I have given her. I am in a good position now to continue to move forward. To give up her father is linked with pain. She is defending against that pain.

This connection with her father was elaborated upon both in fantasies of taking the mother’s place and in sexual fantasies one step removed. She knew the father was interested in strippers and she would fantasize about being a stripper. She would have sexual fantasies about an unidentified man.

She wanted to take the place of her mother. She wanted to be there first, and she wanted to “fill in,” all the while rationalizing why she was doing that, that is, to keep the peace. And, of course, there is the transference issue. Here comes yet another person who wants to get between her and her father. We see the defenses and maneuvers she has used to keep others and herself away from the acknowledgment that her father had a central emotional impact on her life.

We see the germination of the lack of entitlement and self-sabotage from the sadness, guilt, and pain her intrapsychic conflicts have caused her.

11

Pre-Termination of Therapy

The patient comes to the eleventh session and begins with the thought of saying goodbye. Session 10 consolidated the breakthroughs she had made in the ninth session.

At this point introducing termination is evidence of the work she had completed. If she had brought up termination earlier I would have interpreted it as a defensive "flight into health."

In this form of therapy the treatment is over when the work is completed. There are other modalities of brief therapy that set a limit on the number of sessions as another therapeutic tool to bring the patient to resolution. However, for my purposes I have always been more comfortable with the former.

Caroline: I was thinking today, coming here, that this—I hope this is going to end pretty soon.

The patient is introducing termination.

Zois: When you think of it ending, what comes to your mind?

ANXIETY

Caroline: I thought I'm not ready. Then my next thought was, I don't think I'm ever going to be ready. I'm looking for some objective answer to if you're done and sometimes I feel better but sometimes I don't know if I really am.

Zois: So when you think about being done, what comes to your mind?

AMBIVALENCE

Caroline: Being on my own and not feeling finished yet.

Zois: On your own as opposed to?

Caroline: Coming here.

Zois: And being with me?

Caroline: Yeah.

TRANSFERENCE

Caroline introduces the concept of not coming anymore, and believes that she can make it on her own. This has transference implications. She is prepared to give up the past and go on with her life.

When she says "I can make it on my own," she is talking about being able to separate and individuate. It also has implications for the relationship with her husband. The needfulness that caused her problems in the past is now in perspective, and she is relating to him on a more equal plane.

When a patient has come to the point of termination, there will be some anxiety. "It's still sort of scary a little bit": There always will be anxiety at saying goodbye. Termination anxiety is not a reason to continue the therapy. To continue therapy would be to reinforce the notion that if there is any anxiety at all then she is not prepared to terminate.

The termination process actually begins with the first session and evolves throughout treatment. "I can make it on my own. I am ready to say goodbye to you. It's scary." These thoughts are appropriate to the termination process.

The patient states that she has improved, but she has ambivalence and anxiety about ending therapy. For instance, "being on my own and not feeling finished yet." On the one hand there is a part of her that believes she is ready to terminate and continue the work on her own. There is also the other part of her that is anxious. The anxiety has to be interpreted.

The patient casually mentions termination by couching it in terms of "I hope this is going to end soon." This is not an offhand remark. The patient's stream of consciousness is producing material indicating that she is handling her life much better and she can go on without me. The thought of saying goodbye is causing anxiety. That anxiety generates ambivalence and I elect to discuss it in the transference.

Zois: So have you had the thought of saying goodbye to me?

Caroline: Yeah. I didn't think about it for very long.

Zois: What did you think?

INTIMACY

Caroline: Well, part of me said, I don't feel that close to you anyhow, so what difference is it going to make?

This is a defense against intimacy. She goes on to rationalize:

Caroline: And part of me realized that's not really true, but I don't want to think about that. I'll deal with that when the time comes. I'll put it off instead of thinking about it, because all of that besides from feeling finished or not finished or whatever—God, it feels really hot in here to me. Is it? I'm like really—my head feels—it just feels really stifling.

The statement, "God, it feels really hot in here to me," summarizes how she feels about dealing with intimacy and goodbye in the transference.

Zois: Has it felt like this all along?

Caroline: No, no. Probably it's just the time of day. I just am feeling really run down. But it doesn't—I was just thinking it would be nice to have a drink or breath of fresh air or something. I should have gone out for a walk or something. When I thought about that just now, I just thought that it's not allowed or something. I don't know why.

SAYING GOODBYE

Zois: So as you are sitting here and thinking about saying goodbye, you are thinking also about how it's stifling in here.

Caroline: Yeah. Not just that, but closed or something. I think it's just feeling—one day I have a headache from feeling like I just want to sit down and cry and cry all afternoon or something. And I always feel like I'm just going to sit here and fritter away the time and I don't want to do that. I mean, I could very easily just do that.

Again she starts to rationalize as a defense against facing the acknowledgment of the intimate feelings and the pain of saying goodbye. This is very similar to the pain of the goodbye with her father.

Zois: So what are your thoughts about saying goodbye to me? On the one hand you say you don't feel close to me.

Caroline: Well, what I first thought is that I don't want to say goodbye. As much of a hassle as it is, I want to keep coming. I feel like I'm never going to be finished. That's an excuse to keep coming. Plus I just don't like the idea of never seeing you again.

I stay with it and ask for more details.

Zois: What would you miss about me, if you could never see me again?

The discussion about the goodbye is always presented as irrevocable.

Caroline: I don't know. I shouldn't miss you at all. You really put me through the wringer. I wouldn't miss that, but as hard as it might be to believe this, I feel like I can say whatever I have to say, not being judged for it or being any consequences. Even though it's hard for me to do that, I feel like I can do it. It's hard for me to think right now. Maybe it is psychological. My head feels like it's about this big. Well, you have to ask me questions. I don't feel like I can do it.

Zois: So if I don't ask?

Caroline: I'm just going to veg out. I mean waste time. I don't want to do that. I feel like I can answer questions, but I don't feel like I can just freely associate.

Zois: So what you are telling me is that you feel close to me and you can tell me whatever is on your mind.

Caroline: Yes, but I also feel like I need some direction or want some direction.

Zois: So which is it? You need it or you don't?

Caroline: Both. I don't want to waste time, especially if I haven't got that much time left. I don't want to sit here and fritter it away.

Zois: How do you feel right now?

Caroline: I don't know. Every time I say how I feel you say it's not a feeling. Just really exhausted. Like I just want to have to be driven and I can't just do it.

Zois: So when we talk about your saying goodbye to me, the thing you would miss most would be the intimacy, my being able to be close to you?

Caroline: Yeah.

Zois: What else would you miss about me?

Caroline: The process of looking at things instead of just putting them in the corner somewhere and just forgetting they are there, even though that's hard to do.

Zois: What else would you miss about me?

Caroline: Just seeing you. I don't know.

Zois: What is it about me that you would miss?

Caroline: I'm not sure exactly. I don't know.

Zois: Well, think about it. What comes to your mind?

Caroline: All I think about is just seeing you. I don't know. Just being close to you.

Zois: So what would you miss about me?

Caroline: I'm not sure what you mean. You as opposed to the process? I was going to say your supportiveness, but I guess that's a part of the process. I don't know. I don't know if there is a you aside from the process. I can't answer that. I don't think of anything. My mind just kind of goes blank. My whole mind is a blank right now. I guess just being here and just seeing you. I don't have anything else.

Zois: You say, just seeing me, but what about me?

Caroline: I already answered that. Just that you are supportive, that you are there, that you are there helping me. I don't know what you are getting at.

Zois: Well, you have trouble saying goodbye to me, and you say you are going to miss me and I asked you what you are going to miss. On one hand you say you are going to miss talking to me. So what is it you are going to miss about me?

Caroline: I don't know. I can sit here and try to think of something, but nothing pops into my mind. I'm trying to think of it, trying to answer your question, and I can't. I'll just miss seeing you. I'm not getting anywhere with this, am I?

Zois: How do you feel right now?

When the patient has difficulty, examine the emotion in the room.

Caroline: Like I'm not doing what I'm supposed to do.

Zois: How does that feel?

Caroline: Frustrating. I'm kind of avoiding things. I mean, I'm not consciously doing it.

Zois: That's a description. We're talking about saying goodbye to me and you're having difficulty with that.

Caroline: Yes, oh yes. I know that's true, but I don't know how we get to the bottom of it.

Zois: It's difficult to tell me what you are going to miss about me.

Caroline: Yes. That's like when you ask me how angry am I. It's like the same kind of question. I don't know what you mean.

Zois: Yet you say you have had feelings for me?

Caroline: I do. Well, that's why I'll miss seeing you. It may not be the kind of relationship that I would normally associate with that, but it's a relationship. It's almost like I'm not allowed to miss you as a person.

Zois: Where did that idea come from?

Caroline: It's like I don't know you as a person, so how can I miss you as a person? There isn't any relationship there with you as a person. Do you understand what I mean? I mean, you are a person.

Zois: You are saying you are not allowed to—

Caroline: Well, we are supposed to stick to business, and because it's bound to be frustrating. That's why it's not allowed.

Zois: So there is a part of you that holds back.

Caroline: What do you mean?

Zois: When it comes to the thought of missing me, the tender feelings.

Caroline: Yes, yes.

Zois: Because that's not allowed.

Caroline: Yeah.

Zois: So did you hold back that way with your father, the same way, because it wasn't allowed?

Caroline: Yeah. I'm sure I did. He certainly didn't encourage feelings of any kind, tender or whatever. So in some ways it's the same thing, I suppose. Some ways it's not. In some ways, I feel like how can I have any feelings about you because I don't know anything about you?

Zois: So you rationalize why you should not discuss your feelings about me.

Caroline: I know.

Zois: What comes to mind when you think about those tender feelings?

Caroline: I don't know. It makes me feel sad. I'm not sure why. I just sort of feel sad. It's like they are lost or something because it's not reciprocated, or at least that's the way it is in my mind. So it's sort of a waste of time. It's not a waste of time, but it's wasted. It's lost.

I do not become sidetracked by a discussion of reciprocity or "a waste of time" in the transference. Instead I make the connection with her father.

TRIANGLE OF PERSONS

Zois: Can you see parallels with your father?

Caroline: Yeah. I was thinking about that as soon as I said it, that it was wasted on him, too. I'm sitting here and thinking, I know what you are getting at, but I just can't admit it. That I had those feelings for my father, too? I just really have to deny it. I don't feel them at all.

Zois: In your relationship with your father, there was a part of you that wanted to be with him that you deny.

Caroline: Yes.

Zois: There is a part of you that saw your mother absent, the same way that in your mind that Mark is absent.

Caroline: Yes.

Zois: You see you've punished yourself with these thoughts, by isolating yourself, keeping yourself from allowing intimacy with anyone? Then, in a sense, how you've continued this exclusive relationship with your father right down to the letter.

Caroline: You say these are things to work on, but I know—

Zois: These are things that we've discovered.

Caroline: Yeah. I know what you are going to say before I even ask this. How do—I want to work on that, not lose it. I think about it, but is that—

Zois: You see, as you said, these are things you were not thinking about. You had it in your mind somewhere that you wanted to get to these issues the last time.

Caroline: Yes.

Zois: And that you have tried to punish yourself because of these issues, that you've carried this baggage around, that here with me you tend to deal with me the way you've dealt with others.

Caroline: I'm still doing that.

RECAPITULATION

Zois: Now, compare how you were feeling a year ago to now.

Caroline: I don't feel like killing myself.

Zois: How is your mood compared to a year ago?

Caroline: It's a lot better. I don't feel like I get depressed and stay depressed. I feel it's easier for me to deal with people and feel genuinely good about it instead of feeling like I have to put on faces. A good indication of it is that we went to a picnic the other day and there were many people there that I didn't know. I had a real good time. So, that's gotten a lot better.

The session continues with the focus on the triangle of persons and the goodbye in the transference. The patient is the only barometer in determining when the therapy is complete. By the end of this session I can see that Caroline is prepared to deal with the goodbye in the transference and all that it implies. Objectively the work has been done. All of the issues she came to treatment with have been examined. She describes the ways she has improved. The work of terminating is primarily the resolution in the transference.

12

Termination of Therapy

The initial confusion of emotions and material evolves through the therapeutic process into the pattern of a solved jigsaw puzzle. The elements fit into place like a well-told story, with an explanation for all of the components of that story. Caroline has by this time examined all of the problems that have brought her to therapy. The following is the twelfth and final session.

Caroline: I may need those today [looking at a box of tissues]. I feel so much better than I can remember.

Zois: In what way?

RECAPITULATION

Caroline: Well, I feel better toward my husband. I feel a lot closer to him, and I'm able to recover when I lose my temper with my children. I feel happier.

Zois: You say your mood and outlook have improved?

Caroline: I feel better. I could see not coming anymore and feel that it would be all right, that I could make it on my own. It's still scary a little bit.

Zois: As you look at the things that we've discussed here and the way things are, is there anything else that you feel we should be working on?

I ask this question as a way of reinforcing the sense of closure.

Caroline: Well, making decisions. I'm not sure why that's so hard for me. I don't feel like I've gotten very far with that here. I wish I could make a decision about what to do with the rest of my life. My husband and I have been talking about having a baby and I think we might do that.

Zois: The two of you have discussed this and made a decision?

Caroline: Yes.

Zois: What other areas as far as decision making?

Caroline: As far as a career, what I'm going to do when all the kids get into school. And what am I going to be when I grow up. I don't think I'm closer to that now then I was when I graduated from high school.

I do not want to become a career counselor and prolong the treatment.

Zois: In terms of what you want to do with work, that's something you have not dealt with, but the other areas that brought you here, how have those been?

Caroline: Well, those are the only things that I really think about.

Zois: But as far as the issues that brought you here, how have you done with those?

Caroline: Fine.

Zois: Can you review them for me?

Caroline: Well, the biggest thing is my relationship with my children and being able to be more realistic in my expectations and to be calmer with them. Things are starting to improve with my husband. Also I can be more positive and more confident. All in all, things have really changed a lot, for the better.

If this is true then the patient can work on career goals without the help of a psychiatrist.

Zois: So as you look at that, what is the reason not to say goodbye at this time? I see you smile just then.

By phrasing the question in this way the patient has an opportunity to deal with any rationalizations that may exist.

Caroline: Well, mostly I think it's doubting myself and doubting that I'm really ready to do it. I mentioned it to my husband, I said, "I think maybe this could be the last few sessions." And he said, "Don't jump to it." I don't know how he said it exactly. I just don't feel like I need to come anymore, like I used to feel I needed to. I feel like I've dealt with a lot of things that were way down deep there. I guess there isn't any reason not to. It's just that it seems so sudden.

Zois: You say it's "so sudden"?

Caroline: Yeah, I mean, I don't do anything suddenly.

Zois: When did you start to think about saying goodbye?

Caroline: Seriously? Since the last few times I was here. It's like it just suddenly dawned on me that things feel better. Things have been going well and feeling like I can handle things.

Zois: You've been thinking about it for the past few weeks?

Caroline: Yes.

Zois: You have come to the conclusion that things are changed in your life?

Caroline: Yes.

Zois: And the things you came to work on you feel better about?

Caroline: Yes.

Zois: So this idea of "suddenly" gets back to saying goodbye?

Caroline: Yes.

Zois: When you thought about not coming anymore, what came to your mind?

ANXIETY

Caroline: I'm still scared that the depression is going to sneak up on me again when I'm not looking.

What the patient is saying is realistic. This is the first time in a long time that she has felt good. She has accomplished that with help. She asks herself an appropriate question: Without this help, will I continue to feel good, going forward, or will it sneak back?

THE GOODBYE

I have two choices here. I can address that fear and explore it further. I choose instead to continue with the goodbye itself. If I continue talking about the anxieties of saying goodbye rather than looking at the goodbye, I then covertly give her the message that neither one of us can deal with the goodbye.

Zois: So did you have thoughts of saying goodbye to me?

Caroline: Real brief ones. I guess I didn't let myself dwell on that.

Zois: You didn't let yourself dwell on it?

Again she exhibits ambivalence about dealing with the termination.

Caroline: Yeah. I thought I would deal with that when I have to deal with that. It was funny. I said to myself, "This could be one of the last times." And then I said, "I don't think I'm quite ready to do that." Then I thought of in terms of you and not of this thing of depression sneaking up on me.

Zois: What were your thoughts about saying goodbye to me?

Caroline: I don't really let myself think about it that much, because I thought it was something I don't want to do, so I said I wouldn't think about it.

Zois: So as we look at it now, you say it's something that you don't want to do. You don't want to say goodbye to me?

Caroline: Yeah. Well, part of it is not being quite sure about making it on my own.

Zois: So as we look at the thoughts that you may not be able to make it on your own, and the depression will return, in one sense that's another way of saying that you should stay?

Caroline: Yes.

Zois: On the other hand you say you feel that things are changed in your life?

Caroline: Yes.

Zois: Then you introduce this idea that perhaps you shouldn't because things may turn?

Caroline: I think I should feel a little more confident about that before I say, "Yeah, I'm ready. This is it."

Zois: So my question is: The idea that you need to feel more confident, is that related to your reluctance to look at the issue of parting here, the two of us saying goodbye to one another?

Caroline: I'm sure it is.

Zois: Going our separate ways?

Caroline: Um-hmm, yeah.

Zois: How do you feel as you think about that goodbye?

Caroline: I feel really anxious.

I go into the experience of the sadness.

SADNESS IN THE GOODBYE

Zois: How is that? What are you experiencing?

Caroline: I don't know. I just feel a little nervous, sort of tense, and my stomach feels kind of funny. I just feel like I could start crying.

Zois: So you're tearful at the thought of parting?

Caroline: Yes.

She introduces the sadness of the goodbye. Again, this is an appropriate sadness. She has two emotions, the happy feeling at being liberated and the sad feeling of saying goodbye. It is necessary to put these emotions in balance. I do not attempt to erase the emotion that is there. At this point everything she is saying is appropriate to the termination phase. I want her to go away understanding that sadness is part of saying goodbye, that we will say goodbye to one another, we feel sad at saying goodbye, and it's all right to feel that sadness. This is an issue that is frequently overlooked.

Zois: So what comes to your mind?

TRIANGLE OF PERSONS IN THE GOODBYE

Caroline: Well, what just came to my mind was sort of not being able to let go.

The patient next introduces the neurotic transference. She talks about an old boyfriend, and then she talks about her father. She has at this point completed the triangle.

Caroline: I thought specifically about Harry and how hard that was to just kind of let him go. Put things in perspective and saying, that's over, so just let it go. I think I've always had trouble with that. I've had trouble not getting close to somebody knowing that person was going to be gone and just letting that person be gone when they are gone. I always think of my father, too.

Zois: You think about a high school friend and you think about your father, that comes to mind?

Caroline: Yes.

Zois: What about him?

Caroline: Letting them be in the past and somehow let that be all right, that they are in the past.

So much of the work of the previous months has come down to this statement.

Zois: To say goodbye to them?

Caroline: Yes.

Zois: To say goodbye to your father?

Caroline: Yeah, it's funny, at one point a couple of weeks ago I had this thought of going back home. I haven't been home to visit my mother for quite a while, but I had this thought of going home to visit her and going to the cemetery to visit my father's grave. When I thought of that before, I always thought of it in terms of being upsetting, something I didn't want to do or couldn't do. Somehow this time it was different. I saw myself going and I thought that it was all right. It wasn't upsetting. When I think of it it's just like letting him go and letting him be in the past and let that be all right.

Zois: How do you feel right now?

Caroline: I feel very upset about something.

Zois: What comes to your mind?

Caroline: As soon as I come in here I feel like crying.

Zois: So it has to do with being here with me?

Caroline: Yeah.

Zois: You are saying that a couple of weeks ago you had the thought that you could go to your father's grave and say goodbye to him?

Caroline: And what I saw myself say was that it was all right, that things weren't the way I wished they had been, but that's the way it was, and I feel like I have to do that.

The patient has summarized how everyone should be able to deal with loss.

Zois: You say two weeks ago it was clear in your mind, but when you come here then you feel upset about it?

Caroline: Yes.

Zois: So is the upset here about that goodbye which was clear in your mind or about this goodbye?

Caroline: I don't know. I think it is about both [tearful].

THE IRREVOCABLE GOODBYE

Zois: So at the thought that I will be dead for you, you are very tearful?

Caroline: Yes.

Zois: So what comes to your mind?

Caroline: I don't know. I don't want to lose you.

Zois: What are your thoughts about that?

Technically it is important to introduce the goodbye as irrevocable. Frequently when you ask patients how they feel about saying goodbye to you, they will waffle on it, and say, "Well, I know that if I ever have a problem, I can call on you." Now the reality of that may be so, but that is not therapeutically what you want to accomplish.

There are irrevocable goodbyes in the patient's life that she has had to deal with. She has mentioned two: a significant friend and her father. I want to address the resolution of the conflict around her father through the transference by making the termination irrevocable. I do that by including the phrase, "I will be dead for you." In that way I have paralleled the experience with her father. "What if you received a phone call that I had died, how would you react?" is another way of saying this. Here there is no room for her to say, "Well, I can always call you." In this instance it is not necessary to do that, but that is another way technically of introducing the goodbye as irrevocable.

Caroline: I let you be important to me and I'm not sure—how to say goodbye, how to let that go.

I want her to summarize in what ways I have been important.

Zois: In what ways have I been important?

Caroline: Well, you let me face a lot of things that I didn't want to face, that I needed to face. And you listen to a lot of things that I would never be able to say to anybody else that I needed to say. You help me see things in a different way so that I can put things in perspective. It's been a lot of hard work that I didn't want to do. Well, I wanted to get better, but I didn't really want to have to do this to do it.

The experience of the sadness and pain is what the patient is clinging to. She views letting go of these emotions as a betrayal of her memory of her father. She is stating a universal issue. "I want to change my life, but I don't want to face the grief and pain of parting, and I will do whatever is necessary to protect against that."

In the end she is telling me that what she has tried to protect the most is not to feel the pain of the goodbye. Everything she has done in the past has been in the service of protecting against the experience of that pain.

Zois: So that's one area of my being important to you. What else?

Caroline: I don't want to talk. It's all I can think about right now.

Zois: How do you feel about me?

Caroline: How do I feel about you? Well, I don't know if it's a cop-out to say it, but I have a lot of mixed feelings about you.

Zois: What comes to mind?

Caroline: Well, on one hand I feel close to you, because I've told you all of these things, but I let myself feel close to you and yet sometimes I'm really angry at you for putting me through all of this stuff, too, even though I realize that's what I'm here for. I can rationalize it like that, but I still feel—

Zois: So there is that—

Caroline: Some anger.

INTRAPSYCHIC CONFLICT

Again we see a recapitulation of the dilemma. This material is what a patient faces on day one. The patient wants to experience intimacy but does not want to be put through the pain that is linked with closeness, and so marshals the defenses. That is the universal dilemma and conflict in all therapy.

Zois: There is that part of you that sees me as your father, that put you through a lot of pain?

Caroline: Yeah.

Zois: But on the other hand, there are the positive feelings?

Caroline: Yes.

Zois: What are they?

Caroline: I'm not sure. I'm not sure I can verbalize them, I guess [She looks away].

Zois: You are having difficulty looking me in the eyes and telling me what you are thinking about me?

Now we see the return of certain defenses—she looks away.

Caroline: Yeah, because part of it is this rational side of me that keeps saying that I shouldn't have any feelings about you. All that stuff that we've talked about before.

Zois: But we see that you said those same things to yourself about your father.

Caroline: Yes. I still feel that way about him too.

Zois: Now here with me you have trouble telling me those feelings, letting me into those intimate thoughts?

Caroline: Yes. I thought a lot about what we talked about last time, about all of those issues, how to separate feelings for someone from all of those fantasies. I'm conscious of all of that but I'm keeping myself from thinking about it. Even here, even when you ask me, I don't want to think about that.

DREAM OF SUMMATION

The patient relates a dream that is relevant to the termination.

Caroline: I had a dream this morning. In the dream, I'm not sure where I was, but it's supposed to be this limousine comes to pick me and these people up, these other people that I felt close to. I'm not sure who they are until later in the dream. I don't know where we were going or anything, but it wasn't really a limousine. At the time I thought "This is a strange limousine." Afterward, when I thought about it, I thought what it was—it was a hearse. I got in and there were two other people in it. One of them I know, besides the two people, is a driver and another man and someone else I'm not sure who. The association was that it was my father. I was aware that there were three other women getting in the limousine too. But when we got in there were only three of us. There were three seats and three of us. My association to that later was that it was my sisters, four of us, but only three of us actually got in. We started down the road to wherever we were going and I re-

> member feeling really uncomfortable. We were going down the road, and it was cloudy, sort of a stormy day. My father was facing me. All of a sudden I got really scared because I saw what I thought was a tornado. I said, "There's a tornado back there. We have to do something." Everybody looked and they said, "No, that's not a tornado, that's the way the clouds look." For a minute I saw a tornado and I was afraid of it, then I realized it was nothing to be afraid of. It's about that time that I woke up. I had the association when I woke up that the dream was about the sexual feelings about my father. I can see now that whole relationship must have been loaded with that.

This is a dream of summation. The relevant people in her life are there. The tornado is her foreboding about the anxieties, fears, and pain she has had, that they will again envelop her. In the dream she authors someone saying to her, "No, no, it's not a tornado, it's just clouds." In this summation, she is able to see that the bogeymen of the past are nonexistent. She then goes on to talk about things that she had repressed in the past, such as the sexual feelings about her father.

The patient has very few defenses at this point. She produces relevant material that in the past was highly charged, without prodding from me. She is now doing the work herself.

> *Zois:* Now, in the dream when this limousine that was a hearse came to pick you up, where were you?

Again I want to place the patient in the context of the dream, so as to enable her to give as much detail as possible. When I do that, she recalls that there were two men in the front seat and that there was some kind of joking. Technically, as we discussed before, I ask the patient to repeat the dream a second time. She does and then I ask questions about it, eliciting more detail.

Caroline: In a parking lot somewhere. I remember a lot of cars and I could just see the top of this, what I thought was a limousine. As soon as I saw it I realized that it wasn't a limousine because it had a distinctive shape.

Zois: There was a driver?

Caroline: Yeah.

Zois: Then somebody next to him?

Caroline: Yes, somebody else in the front seat with him. I remember them joking or something, I don't recall about what.

Zois: They were joking about something?

Caroline: They were happy or light-hearted. I was surprised or thought that it was inappropriate because the occasion seemed to be very somber. I don't know where I was going but it wasn't a happy occasion. When the limousine, or hearse, got there everyone was inside except the driver and the person in the front seat with him.

Zois: Now, the man who you associated with your father, where was he sitting?

Caroline: Across from me.

Zois: Did you speak with him?

Caroline: I don't think so. My feeling is that I was just so intimidated and unsure of myself that I didn't say anything. I was going to wait for him to say something.

Zois: You were intimidated by him?

Caroline: Yeah.

Zois: Where did you go in this hearse?

Caroline: We just went down the road someplace.

Zois: What was it like? You say you looked out the window.

Caroline: It was real flat.

Zois: Real flat?

Caroline: Yes, it was like home.

Zois: It was similar to where you grew up?

Caroline: Yeah. It looked like that. You could see forever and all you could see was trees.

Zois: Then you saw these cloud formations that you thought were tornadoes?

Caroline: Yes.

Zois: And you explained that you had seen a tornado?

Caroline: Yes.

Zois: In your dream you remember explaining something that happened?

Caroline: Yes.

Zois: Who told you that they were not tornadoes?

Caroline: I think my father did. I remember he turned around.

Zois: What did he say?

Caroline: He said something like, "No, that's not a tornado. It's not anything to worry about."

Zois: You were anxious that there would be this tornado?

Caroline: Yes.

Zois: And he allayed your anxiety?

Caroline: Um-hmm.

Zois: Then where did you come to stop?

Caroline: We didn't. I just woke up. The feeling was that we were still going somewhere and it was someplace that I wasn't sure I wanted to go.

I interpret the dream in terms of saying goodbye to her father, going to visit the grave.

Zois: Where is the place that you didn't want to go that you were thinking about earlier?

Caroline: I don't know.

Zois: When you came in and told me you were thinking about your father, where did you say you wanted to go then?

Caroline: To visit his grave.

Zois: Then in the dream there is this place that you don't want to go. So in the dream you're taking your father to the cemetery and as you are going there you are anxious. He tells you, "It's all right." That's the way it was in this dream, wasn't it?

Caroline: Yes.

Zois: This voice from the grave is telling you it's all right to put him to rest?

Caroline: Yes.

Again, the interpretation toward the resolution of the inability to let go, to say goodbye.

Zois: For your part, you still have some anxiety, but he reassures you?

Caroline: Yes.

Zois: What is his attitude in the dream?

Caroline: It was funny. If I think of it now, it wasn't like my father at all, I mean, to be very reassuring and—

Zois: His attitude in the dream is that he's very reassuring?

Caroline: Yes. He was saying that everything is all right, whereas in reality that wouldn't have been that way at all.

Zois: But in the dream he's more the father you wanted?

Caroline: Yes.

Zois: And he's giving you permission to say goodbye to him?

Caroline: Yes.

In the dream the father is the male ideal, the father the patient had wanted. This issue is common in treatment. The parents were not all the patient wanted them to be. There is not only the sense of being victimized but the sense of regret and the sense of not having received what the patient imagines she should have gotten. She is struggling to attain the realization that in order to be free of the past she has to accept certain negatives as a part of life. I bring it into the moment.

Zois: How do you feel now as you think about that?

Caroline: I feel like I could just sit here and cry for the rest of the afternoon. But I also feel relieved. But I also feel like I'm not really sure that I can believe that. I want to, but I don't know.

Zois: There is a part of you that wants to hang on to the old way?

Caroline: No, I don't. I'm just so used to that.

I return to the transference.

Zois: This thought that you are not sure you can believe it, it's similar to the thought that maybe the depression will come back when you think about saying goodbye to me?

Caroline: Yes.

Zois: So this part of you that is still holding on to me—

Caroline: Yes.

Zois: Can we look at that?

Caroline: I think you were in that car too.

Zois: In the dream you are prepared to say goodbye to both of us.

Caroline: In the dream.

Zois: You say, "in the dream." So you were thinking about saying goodbye to us?

Caroline: I'm just not sure.

Zois: There is that part of you that wants to hold on.

Caroline: Yeah.

Every time the patient says she is not sure, my interpretation is, "So you want to hold on." The "I'm not sure" is the ambivalence, and I always address that ambivalence by interpreting that she wants to hold on. Next, I use the word "final" purposely.

Zois: As you think about our final goodbye, how do you feel?

Caroline: I just feel really mixed up about it. Part of me feels that I don't feel confident about things. I'm just not sure that I can do it by myself. A part of me doesn't want to leave, because coming here has made me feel better and I feel close to you because you've helped me.

Zois: How do you experience the feelings of closeness?

Caroline: Gratitude. It's great that you have patience to sit here and listen to all of this and to help me work through it.

Zois: How do you feel toward me?

Caroline: I just had the thought to say that I love you, but I don't know—that's—that feels uncomfortable to say that.

Zois: You're anxious telling me about your tender feelings towards me.

TENDER FEELINGS

The patient is saying, "I feel close to you because you've helped me." That is not transference. Those are tender, authentic feelings toward me for having been helpful. That distinction is important. The transference deals with what she was talking about before, seeing me as someone like the father she can not say goodbye to. *That* is the neurotic issue she has to resolve. However, I have to acknowledge the authenticity of the feelings the patient experiences for having been helped. When she says to me she thinks that she loves me, she is uncomfortable with that emotion because of the sexual connotation. Rather than explore the sexual connotation of that feeling of love, it is important to clarify instead for the patient that these are the tender feelings that have arisen as a result of therapy. The interpretation when the patient says, "I have the thought I love you but I feel uncomfortable," is to say, "You're anxious telling me about your tender feelings toward me."

Caroline: I'm anxious to tell you. I feel anxious when I tell you, yes. The same way I would have felt to tell my father that—anxious.

Zois: How do you feel this minute when you look me in my eyes and tell me what you feel?

Caroline: It's a lot easier than I thought it would be. I guess that means I'm getting ready to say goodbye. When I thought about making this the last day I was having that feeling that I had to admit things to myself, and to you. I feel a lot better now that I've said that. I still feel anxious and have the thought that I shouldn't have said that.

Zois: What comes to your mind?

Caroline: That I shouldn't admit how I feel about things.

Zois: About things?

Caroline: I give that to myself.

Zois: You mean about me?

Caroline: Yes. About you.

Zois: You are comfortable with the experiences of the tender feelings that in your mind I have been helpful to make you feel better?

TRIANGLE OF PERSONS IN PERSPECTIVE

Caroline: I think I do that with a lot of things. I do that with Mark. It's hard for me to feel close to him because I just haven't been able to admit how I feel about him. I haven't been able to feel that closeness for some reason. I want to push it away and not let it be there.

Zois: How are things between the two of you now?

Caroline: They're better.

Zois: In what ways?

Caroline: The most obvious thing is that we make love more often than we have been and I've felt better about it. The last time we made love it was more like it used to be. It was fun and I felt really close to him. I felt that he felt really close to me too. It was just like I wish it were all the time.

Zois: When was that? When was the last time you made love?

Caroline: Last weekend. I initiated things and everything was terrific. I felt good about it. It surprised me later when I realized that instead of withdrawing I had gotten closer to him. I felt differently. I felt like doing little things for him. I just felt so close to him, closer than I have in a long time. Things have gotten better, but I don't know if it will last.

The memory of her father no longer comes between her and her husband. With the resolution of the relationship with her father comes an increased and enhanced ability to become close to her husband. There is a correlation between her ability to relate to her spouse and her ability to put her father in perspective and say goodbye to him.

When she again says "I don't know if it will last" that is the trigger for me. She puts me on notice to return to the transference. Again I interpret this as a defense rather than as having anything to do with the relationship with her husband. I know that the memory of her father is improved, and therefore I am on solid ground to move forward and return to the goodbye in the transference. Technically, again and again I reiterate our final goodbye.

Zois: Again, a thought comes to mind that you are not ready to say goodbye to me?

Caroline: No. I don't think I've ever been 100 percent sure of anything in my life. That's the whole thing about making up my mind about things, what I want to do with the rest of my life and things like that. I've never been able to say, "Hey, this is it," and "That's what I want," and to do it. I've just never felt sure enough of myself to do that.

Zois: So here with me, now, it's the same thing?

Caroline: Yeah.

Zois: What will it be like when we say our final goodbye in your mind? How do you feel about that?

Caroline: I feel like I'll probably be all right, but—

Zois: You say you'll "probably be all right." But what's the feeling?

Caroline: Like I said before, I have really mixed feelings about it.

Zois: How do you feel right now about what you're saying?

Caroline: I'm not sure exactly how to describe it. I feel like I don't necessarily. . . . I want to, but I guess that will be all right.

Zois: What's the feeling?

Caroline: I'm not sure.

Zois: So you have difficulty?

Caroline: Yeah. I'm not sure exactly what you're looking for. I'm not ready to get up and say, "Well, 'bye." But I feel like I can. I think that I really wish it could be the last time and yet when I think that I think, no.

Zois: What are your thoughts about that?

Caroline: As I said before, it's starting to seem like it's more of a hassle than it's worth.

Zois: As we talk about saying goodbye, that's a hassle?

Caroline: Yes.

Zois: We see that you are having difficulty telling me how you feel about saying goodbye to me, that this was a problem that you had with your father.

Caroline: Yes.

Zois: What are your thoughts now?

Caroline: It is a hassle.

Zois: How do you feel about that?

Caroline: In a way I'm sort of annoyed, like I don't really need to do this anymore. I would like to believe that.

Zois: You tell yourself you are annoyed?

Caroline: In a way, yes.

Zois: You say "in a way." *So is it easier for you to be angry than it is to say goodbye?*

Caroline: No, I don't think so.

Zois: That's how you dealt with your father. In your mind you stayed angry in lieu of saying good-bye.

So there is a part of you that wants to do this with me.

Caroline: No, I don't think so.

Zois: You say you are annoyed?

Caroline: Yeah, I'm annoyed.

Zois: We're talking about saying goodbye and you're telling me you are annoyed.

Caroline: [appears sad] Yes.

Zois: What will it be like to say goodbye to me?

Caroline: Part of me will be relieved that I won't have to do this anymore.

Zois: That's a description. That doesn't tell me how you feel about saying goodbye to me.

Caroline: Well, I told you before, I have mixed feelings about it.

Zois: What are those feelings?

Caroline: The negative side is not being sure I can do it on my own, feeling like some day I might need you and you won't be there. And feeling glad that you've helped me as much as you have.

Zois: That's not a feeling about saying goodbye to me.

Caroline: I think it is. Then it's a semantic difference or something.

Zois: You want to talk about these other things, but you don't want to talk about saying goodbye to me and how you feel about that.

Caroline: I'm trying to talk about it. I am.

Zois: You haven't told me your feelings as you think about saying goodbye.

Caroline: I probably will feel partly sad and partly glad.

Zois: You say you will "probably feel sad"?

Caroline: I don't know. When it happens then I'll know.

Zois: But it's here. We're talking about it. How do you feel about the way you are here in the process of saying goodbye to one another?

Caroline: Partly sad and partly glad. Is that a feeling?

Zois: Tell me about the sadness.

Caroline: I don't know if I can. I mean, not in terms that you want me to.

Zois: So?

Caroline: What?

Again she becomes defensive. I point out that she is putting up a wall.

Zois: You're pulling back from me.

Caroline: No, I'm just not sure. I've told you already that I'm not sure.

Zois: As you tell me about the sadness, how do you feel right now?

Caroline: Sad.

Zois: You look tearful?

Caroline: Yes, I am.

Zois: You are looking down.

Caroline: Yes, so part of me feels sad.

Zois: You say that just now almost as if you are embarrassed by it or want to dismiss it.

I address her defense of attempting to minimize it, which is the defense of avoidance.

Caroline: Yes. Yes, I want to think about positive things. I don't want to try to think about the negative aspect of it, that I may not be able to do it.

Zois: May not be able to do what?

Caroline: Survive.

Zois: Because the feelings are too painful?

Caroline: Yes.

Zois: How do you feel about that?

Caroline: I guess sad.

Zois: You say you guess you are sad. Are you?

Caroline: Yes.

Zois: How sad are you?

Caroline: Very sad. It gets back to saying goodbye.

Zois: You say there is a part of you that's sad to say goodbye?

Caroline: Yes. You've been a big part of my life for quite a while.

Zois: So when we do say goodbye, then you go your way and you take a part of me with you.

Caroline: Yes.

Zois: And I go mine and I take a part of you with me.

Caroline: Yeah.

It is always important to make this statement to the patient because that is what all relationships that have ended have in common—the ability to take what has been positive about the relationship and allow it to enrich your life as you go forward and meet other people. In the best sense, our past relationships, with their positives and their negatives, should leave us with what has been redeeming, what has been inspiring. It is that sense of fulfillment that we take with us when we form other relationships.

THE PAIN OF THE GOODBYE

I go back to the idea that it is normal to feel the pain of saying goodbye.

Zois: On one level that makes you feel sad that our time together has come to an end.

Caroline: It's funny, because I had the thought that now that I'm better, it seems a shame that we have to say goodbye.

Zois: What comes to your mind?

Caroline: I think it's a special relationship here. It's not normal. I feel like I've come here and, it's funny when you say "take a part of me." My thought was that it's too bad that it has to be all of this pain and all of that stuff instead of what I'm really like.

Zois: How would you describe yourself?

Caroline: That's funny. The first word that came to my mind was free. Maybe that's a little too dramatic. Happier, more confident. I'm not ready to set the world on fire, but I'll get there some day. I feel better. I feel—it's funny. I'm sitting here feeling like I'm going to cry and I don't know why.

Zois: What comes to your mind?

Caroline: The thought that I might not be coming back again.

Zois: So you do know why, but it's difficult to look at that?

Caroline: Yes.

We have gone from the discussion of "perhaps I will say goodbye" and some of the mild defensiveness to a recapitulation of many of the relevant issues that the treatment has addressed.

Yet, even here, in saying "might," she still holds on a little bit to the impulse that it is not good to say goodbye, that it hurts too much. However, she hangs on only in a small way. The defenses are now minimal.

In continuing, I say "that this *is* our last time," without even addressing the "might." The patient then shows emotion in the room.

Zois: As you have this thought that this is our last time, how do you feel?

Caroline: Oh, I'm starting to cry. Sad. I feel like I'm going to miss you, but I'm not going to miss coming here and tearing my guts out.

Zois: What will you miss about me?

Caroline: I'm not sure. Just you being there.

Zois: As you think about it?

Caroline: The fact that you are there even though I'm tearing my guts out. I mean, the fact that you were there and the fact that you helped. Even my own mother wouldn't do that. Even my husband couldn't do that. So it's a very special relationship. There is sadness at the end. It's hard to just walk away and say, "That's the end of it." I think I can do it if I have it in the back of my mind that I can always come back. I mean, it's not really goodbye.

Zois: The idea of this final goodbye makes you sad?

Caroline: Yes. I was thinking, "Well, maybe I can come just one more time and then that will be easier." But now it wouldn't. I will still have to say goodbye whether it's now or later. It's not going to be any easier then.

Zois: As you think about it, what is it that you would want to do? Say goodbye today or say goodbye at a later time?

Caroline: I'd rather do it today.

Zois: Last time we reviewed the issues in your life that brought you here and how those issues have changed.

Caroline: Yes.

Zois: Your moods have changed. Your relationship with your husband has changed?

Caroline: Yes.

Zois: Your relationship with your children has improved?

Caroline: Yes. I'm not suicidal anymore.

Zois: You don't have thoughts of suicide?

Caroline: No.

Zois: And that your father is in a different perspective for you?

Caroline: Yes.

She is able to say about him what she is able to say about most of the important relationships in her past life: "It's not the way I wanted it to be totally, but that's the way it was." One of the cornerstones of mental health is the ability to look at the regrets and unfinished business of the past, and say, "That's the way it was."

Caroline: Can we do it today?

Zois: How do you feel about that?

Caroline: Okay, I think.

Zois: What's "I think"?

Caroline: Well, that's just my usual doubt creeping in. I really just want to. This sounds wrong, but I just want to get it over with.

Zois: You say "it sounds wrong"?

Caroline: It sounds like it's an ordeal. In a way it is.

Zois: How do you feel right now?

Caroline: First thing I was going to say, this isn't a feeling, you are going to say, but I can get up and leave right now and say, "That's it." I mean, I think I might as well just do it. Like I can do it. That's how I feel right now: I should do it while I have the feeling, before it escapes me.

Zois: There is again hesitation?

Caroline: Yes.

Zois: Carrying through?

Caroline: Yes.

Zois: Which is another way of saying, it's difficult to say goodbye?

Caroline: Yes. We've established that. I can remember sometimes coming here and just feeling very acutely aware there is something there and I don't feel that way anymore.

Zois: We see in the dream, with reassurance, you are talking with your father and me about a final goodbye.

Again I interpret the dream. I present the anxiety as appropriate.

Caroline: Yes. Somehow it seems like it should be harder than that.

Zois: Harder than this?

Caroline: Yes, especially with my father. I mean, to have that dream and to talk about it and then, that's it.

Zois: So on one hand you thought it was very painful over these weeks to talk about, and on the other hand you are saying you were able to do it?

Caroline: It seems like it's something that was so ominous, that it couldn't be dispelled, sort of. That's how I felt here last time.

She talks about the pre-termination. We see the work that was done and the work that she continued to do on her own. The dream is evidence that she was working on the goodbye from the last session.

Caroline: I felt it was this big dark cloud that had just lifted. When I got home it took me a while before I could talk to Mark about that session. He asked me, "How did it go?" And I said I didn't really want to talk about it. The next day when we did get a chance to talk about it, it was really hard for me to do it.

Zois: What is it that you told him?

Caroline: The thing I remember the most is talking about the fantasy about you and that was just really hard to talk to him about: When I actually started to talk to him about it, it wasn't all that bad. And all of the things about when I had taken my mother's place. After I talked to him I started feeling better about things. It was like this big cloud was lifted. It was something that was just there for years and years and suddenly it goes away. It seems too good to be true.

Caroline discusses her increased ability to accomplish intimacy with her husband. She is able to overcome her lifelong difficulty sharing her innermost thoughts.

Caroline: So what else do we have to do now? Is there a process or anything to this? I mean it's funny. I was thinking about the other time I was in therapy. It started out once a week for maybe six months, but then it was twice a week, and went on for a total of three and a half years. As I say, it really didn't—when I terminated therapy, it took a lot longer, going twice a week for an hour, and it all just seemed very indefinite. It's partly because I was quitting before I was finished.

Zois: It seemed indefinite then?

Caroline: Yeah. We just kind of wound down. I stopped going, but it didn't feel like I was finished. It was, I think I wasted a lot of time.

Zois: In what way?

Caroline: It wasn't that confrontational and making me face things. One day I said, "Goodbye" and that was it. I didn't feel like I had really resolved anything.

Zois: Had you discussed leaving any time prior to that?

Caroline: Some, but not a lot. It was just so different. This has been so different. When I look back at that I say, "Why do they even bother doing it that way anymore when you can do it this way and be so much more productive?" I look back at that now as a total waste of time. This whole process has been real, it seemed to have a definite track.

Zois: How did you feel after you left that therapist? How did you feel about saying goodbye to him?

I continue to focus on the goodbye and not on her complaints about the shortcomings of her previous therapist.

Caroline: I missed him for a while. This was twice a week for so long. I didn't feel that close to him. I liked him and I think he did as good a job as he could do. It was nice to have somebody to go and talk to, understanding, to listen and not be judgmental. I don't think he helped me that much, so I don't feel that close to him.

Zois: What was the difference between that experience then and this experience now?

Caroline: I can answer that in a lot of different ways. I don't really think I faced anything with him. I don't think I worked through anything, resolved anything. I don't think I stopped doing any of the destructive things that I was doing. I went through the whole experience without having any insights into anything. I know I was just very defensive and very resistant. It wasn't geared toward breaking it down. I don't think I ever had to face anything in there. I really think here in this therapy, it was the confrontation and all of that, that really made the difference.

Zois: You say "confrontation"?

Caroline: Yeah. I can sit and, as you know, resist all day. Let me do it and I'll do it. And that's what I did. He would let me do it. When I think about it now, it really makes me angry. I know that was the technique and that was supposed to happen but I just wasted a lot of time, not to mention money. It was just totally different. I remember after the first time I was in here, I said, "I made more progress in one session here than I did in three and a half years in that therapy." The biggest difference was how I felt when I finished. So tell me what I have to do before I can leave. What are the requirements?

Zois: Is there anything that you want to do or say before you leave?

Caroline: Just, "thank you," I feel like that's not enough, really. I don't know what else I could say. It all seems, for you to do what you've done is pretty incredible. I mean, to say thank you isn't really enough.

Zois: How do you feel now as you are telling me these things?

Caroline: I feel like I'm going to cry again. You have done a lot for me, and to acknowledge that and just walk out is hard.

Zois: You say "to acknowledge it and just walk out"?

Caroline: Yes.

Zois: What comes to your mind when you say "just walk out"?

Caroline: It seems like there should be something more I could say because in a lot of ways, I really feel like you've saved my life. And to just say thank you somehow isn't enough. It's hard for me to even acknowledge that, because I want to say, well, it wasn't that way, but it was. I just feel like crying. I wish I could understand why I feel like that.

Zois: What comes to your mind when you think about it?

Caroline: The first thing that comes to my mind is realizing that it's really over, that you are not saying "Wait a minute. You don't think you're ready to leave, do you?" I know that I want you to reassure me that's the right thing to do. I know it's something that I have to decide and I guess if I weren't ready you would tell me.

Zois: You say you "guess I would tell you"? So there is still some doubt in your mind?

Caroline: Well, a little bit. I guess I want you to say "No, don't go."

Zois: You are thinking that I would say because you are not done or that I would demonstrate to you that I also have feelings for you?

Caroline: Both. Both, but mainly the latter. Like I said, I didn't really think about that, what I mean to you. If I did think about it, that I didn't really matter to you, I mean, that's just my defense though.

Zois: So as you are leaving, how do you want me to see you, in your mind?

Caroline: It's hard to say. It's hard to put into words. Sometimes I'm thinking, but I can't say it. That I'm competent. It's funny, because I can see a time when I would have said that and I would have felt a real split or something there, but I don't mean it that way. Coming here and having all of this garbage, you know, that's not really how I am. It's just the negative side of me and I have a positive side too. I can say that now. I don't think I felt so sure about saying that when I first came in here, that there was another side of me for anyone to know.

Zois: As far as someone only seeing one side of you, was it true with anyone else?

Caroline: Anytime you ask me something like that, the answer is always my father, because that's just what I thought of. That's partly because I only saw one side of him. I see that now. For so long I tried to be the way he wanted me to be. The other side of me was so buried. I was thinking about whether he would appreciate me now the way I am instead of being his helpless little girl who could never do anything right. I feel like you should be asking me a lot of questions.

Zois: What kind of questions?

Caroline: Questions to see whether I'm really ready to leave or not.

Zois: Such as?

Caroline: I don't know. You've already asked me a lot of questions.

Zois: You indicate that you still have doubt that you should leave.

Caroline: I don't have doubts until. . . . If this is going to be the end, are there things that I should be thinking about?

Zois: What comes to your mind?

Caroline: Nothing comes to my mind. You know, you're the one with the questions.

Zois: What do you think about in your mind?

Caroline: What leaving here means, but we already talked about that. I don't know if I've covered the territory or not. I just feel like you probably know what questions I need to answer.

Zois: You return to this idea that there is something undone. Is that so?

Caroline: I feel like there is, like things that I should remember. If I start to feel really low again, I can think about. I feel like you see those things a lot more clearly than I do. I get mired down in all of the feelings that you can see more clearly. When you said I wanted to take my mother's place with my father it was obvious, but it wasn't that obvious to me. It was obvious to you because you weren't feeling those feelings. Things like that. Because I just get bogged down.

Zois: Do you feel bogged down now?

Caroline: Yeah.

Zois: In what area?

Caroline: Leaving here. That's what we've been talking about. It's funny. I want to be able to just—I feel like I should be able to just say, "Okay, goodbye." And I feel like if I'm really better I would be able to do that instead of sitting here feeling like I'm going to cry all afternoon.

Zois: What do you want to cry about?

Caroline: Not wanting to leave you.

Zois: So again there is sadness at that part?

Caroline: Yes.

Zois: There is a part of you that would like to avoid those feelings?

Caroline: Yes, I feel if I were really better, I would just be able to do that.

Zois: But you see with your father you tried to avoid the feelings and dismiss them.

Caroline: Yes.

Zois: But that, in fact, you were carrying a lot of feelings about him.

Caroline: Yes.

Zois: So here with me you acknowledge those feelings.

Caroline: Yes.

Zois: Is there anything else that you wanted to tell me about saying goodbye to me?

Caroline: Not that I'm conscious of. I don't think of anything. It seems like there should be—after all this time and all of this stuff that somehow it should be a ceremony or something, I mean, a diploma of mental health or something. I just walk out and leave. That's what I was saying before. Just to say thank you isn't enough. I think that's why I want to put it off until the next time, then I could make this big deal out of it, make it final in my own mind.

Zois: How is it in your mind now?

Caroline: It's getting there. It's getting there. Because I feel there might be all of these things that I'll think of when I leave, "Oh, I should have talked about this." Or "I should have talked some more about that." But I guess I can deal with them on my own. I almost feel like if I had known this was going to be the last time I would have had this little checklist in my mind. But we've talked about a check-off list and I have everything checked off, except this career decision. Anyway.

Zois: What are your thoughts?

Caroline: Every other time I left here, it was always all of this heavy stuff I'm carrying, and trying to remember it so I could think about it and try to work with it. I always got back home feeling like I was really dragged out. I don't feel like it today. But it's funny because I'm thinking, well, that's what I'm here for.

Zois: What are your thoughts?

Caroline: Just how to say goodbye. I've had this thing in my mind, I know you are not a real person, I mean, you just sit here and listen to all of this stuff. My thought was, how do I say it? I'll just do it. This is terrible. Whether I just shake hands like with somebody that I'm in business with or whether I give you a hug, because you are somebody I've been close to that I have feelings about. I was thinking, well, if I was really better, I wouldn't be so formal. But then I started thinking, that's not really proper. It's like saying thank you just doesn't seem to be enough. It's just so formal and businesslike and everything is supposed to be businesslike, isn't it? That's my conflict.

Zois: So if you were to shake hands with me it would be like a business meeting?

Caroline: Yeah, and after I left I would think that was really dumb, but it would also have been the safest thing to do, because it's the most conservative of what I would be like. I can't find fault with that.

Zois: So your dilemma is do you hug me and show me that you care about me or shake my hand and not be sure that you have shown me that you care about me?

Caroline: Right. Right, exactly. You say it so much easier than I do. It's so much easier when you say it.

Zois: It is?

Caroline: Yes. I feel like the old me would just want to be businesslike and the new me would. . . . I don't know.

Zois: There is in your mind the thought that you haven't shown me how you feel about me at this moment, that it hinges on your shaking hands or hugging me?

Caroline: Not that it hinges on that, it's the last time I'm going to see you, so that's significant in my mind. It's the same old dilemma, what I have with my father about showing affection to him. I never did, much. I don't remember ever showing him that much affection. I wish I had because I realize now I do have feelings for my father that just were so far out of touch.

This exchange encompasses two issues. The first has implications for how she viewed herself in the past. The question is: Is she enough for someone who has been good to her or to whom she feels she owes a debt, or does she have to give something more than her tender feelings? You will see many cases in which the belief that a person is not enough leads to sexual acting out that is really in the service of attempting to feel a sense of completeness rather than authentic emotions. It is based on insecurities and a lack of confidence. She raises this dilemma and I confront her on it.

FOLLOW-UP

Caroline: I'm going to miss coming here. As hard as it's been, for this long I've had this to count on if something is bothering me, I can say I'll save it until I come here, but I'm going to have to do it on my own. I think I can do it. If not, I guess I can always come back for a check up or something, right?

Zois: We will have a six-month follow-up, if that's acceptable to you.

I have already dealt with the irrevocable goodbye previously. Here it is not necessary to delve into that issue.

Caroline: Fifty thousand mile tune-up or something. Okay.

Zois: We can make it in the spring.

Caroline: Okay. It seems like a long time. I'm sitting here thinking, gee, is there anything that I wanted to, you know, speak now or forever hold your peace. I can't think of anything. You don't think of anything, do you? I guess not or you would ask me. I really can't believe this is it. It's still sort of scary. It's also sort of exhilarating. I'm thinking of going home and getting a bottle of champagne to celebrate mental health. I feel really torn. I feel like I should talk about something significant or talk about the weather.

Zois: What comes to your mind?

Caroline: Nothing. Nothing. I just blank out. I don't think of anything heavy. I'm sitting here trying to think, oh, let's just talk. Well, this is a whole new thing. I don't know if I can do that. What I think of doing now is sort of meeting you for the first time, so nothing comes to mind. That's the trouble. I feel like I'm blank. I think I should just go. I don't want to do that though. It's my last chance. I want to say goodbye to you. I don't think I'm going to be able to decide. I'm sitting here obsessed about it. So what should we do? I'm supposed to decide that, right? I don't want to decide that. I want you to decide whether we should be serious or not serious. I feel really anxious now.

Zois: What is it that you are anxious about?

Caroline: I'm not sure, besides saying goodbye. That, mostly. And this is my last chance.

Zois: You repeated that a few times. When you say your "last chance" what do you mean?

Caroline: Wanting to feel sure that I can sort of make it on my own and that I don't really need you there to wrap me up.

Zois: In the end who is in the best position to determine that?

Caroline: I am.

Caroline clearly illustrated how guilt, anger and a sense of victimization from the past resulted in passivity, depression, and self-sabotage in her current life. The therapy was successful in large part by working with the intimacy in the transference. This enabled her to move past her defenses and free herself from the emotions engendered by a skewed view of her mother and father. Through the continuous use of challenge and focus the therapy gave her the tools that allowed her to come to terms with the distorted images and impulses. Caroline completed treatment in twelve sessions. On six month and two-year follow-up she had no recurrence of the symptoms that brought her to therapy.

Summary and Conclusion

The case histories and transcripts that are presented in this text are meant to convince therapists that psychotherapy is a straightforward process. Patients present with universal issues. In spite of the multiplicity of theories, these cases illustrate that there are only a handful of issues that represent the "final common pathways" for a potentially infinite number of human experiences.

Moreover, therapists must understand that to address these issues effectively, treatment technique must be straightforward, sequential, and relentlessly focused on resistance. Generous use of the transference is the oil that keeps the psychotherapeutic engine running smoothly. Therapist appreciation for the pain involved in loss in the transference and countertransference will ensure that termination fulfills the requirements necessary for a successful conclusion. Remember: the termination not only prepares the patient to end therapy but to begin to live a life without the pain and burden of the past. Termination recapitulates the pain of past goodbyes in the transference. This process is played out repeatedly throughout the treatment. In a sense, termination begins with the first session. The psychotherapist who appreciates this will have an easier time constructing a mental image of a road map of the therapy. Layered over this map is the short-term technique.

This book is not intended as a definitive text on how to do therapy. It is meant to inspire clinicians to evolve and improve upon the theories and techniques of insight-oriented psychotherapy. The primary motivation of the therapist should always be the alleviation of the patient's suffering in the shortest possible time. I hope that this book will help accomplish that goal.

Bibliography

Alexander, F., and French, T. M. (1946). *Psychoanalytic Therapy: Principles and Applications.* New York: Ronald.

Alpert, M. (1996). Videotaping psychotherapy. *Journal of Psychotherapy Practice and Research* 5:93–105.

Armstrong, S. (1980). Dual focus in brief psychodynamic psychotherapy. *Psychotherapy and Psychosomatics* 33:147–154.

Balint, M., Ornstein, P., and Balint, E. (1972). *Focal Psychotherapy: An Example of Applied Psychoanalysis.* London: Tavistock.

Barten, H. H. (1969). The coming of age of the brief psychotherapies. In *Progress in Community Health,* ed. L. Bellak and H.H. Barten. New York: Grune & Stratton.

Bauer, G. (1993a). *The Analysis of the Transference in the Here and Now.* Northvale, NJ: Jason Aronson.

——— (1993b). *Brief Therapy*. Northvale, NJ: Jason Aronson.

Bellak, L., and Small, L. (1978). *Emergency Psychotherapy and Brief Psychotherapy*. New York: Grune & Stratton.

Berger, D. (1987). *Clinical Empathy*. Northvale, NJ: Jason Aronson.

Budman, S. H., ed. (1981). *Forms of Brief Therapy*. New York: Guilford.

Budman, S. H., and Gurman, A. S. (1983). The practice of brief therapy. *Professional Psychology: Research and Practice* 14:277–292.

Butcher, J. H., and Koss, M. P. (1978). Research of brief and crisis-oriented psychotherapies. In *Handbook of Psychotherapy and Behavior Change*, 2nd ed., ed. S. L. Garfield and A. E. Bergin. New York: Wiley.

Castelnuovo-Tedesco, P. (1975). Brief psychotherapy. In *American Handbook of Psychiatry*, 2nd ed., vol. 5, ed. S. Arieti. New York: Basic Books.

Davanloo, H., ed. (1978). *Basic Principles and Techniques in Short-Term Dynamic Psychotherapy*. New York: Spectrum.

——— ed. (1980). *Short-Term Dynamic Psychotherapy*. New York: Jason Aronson.

Firestein, S. (1978). *Termination in Psychoanalysis*. New York: International Universities Press.

Frank, J. D., Hoehn-Saric, S. D., Imber, B., et al. (1978). *Effective Ingredients of Successful Psychotherapy*. New York: Brunner/Mazel.

Freud, A. (1936). *The Ego and the Mechanisms of Defense*. London: Hogarth.

Freud, S. (1937). Analysis terminable and interminable. *Standard Edition* 23:216–253.

Gill, M. M. (1982). *Analysis of Transference I: Theory and Technique*. New York: International Universities Press.

Gustafson, J. P. (1981). The complex secret of brief psychotherapy in the work of Malan and Balint. In *Forms of Brief Therapy*, ed. S. H. Budman. New York: Guilford.

Kernberg, O. F. (1975). *Borderline Conditions and Pathological Narcissism.* New York: Jason Aronson.

——— (1976). *Object Relations Theory and Clinical Psychoanalysis.* New York: Jason Aronson.

Malan, D. H. (1963a). *A Study of Brief Psychotherapy.* New York: Plenum.

——— (1963b). *The Frontier of Brief Psychotherapy.* New York: Plenum.

——— (1976). *Toward the Validation of Dynamic Psychotherapy: A Replication.* New York: Plenum.

——— (1979). *Individual Psychotherapy and the Science of Psychodynamics.* London: Butterworth.

Mann, J. (1973). *Time-Limited Psychotherapy.* Cambridge, MA: Harvard University Press.

Mann, J., and Goldman, R. (1982). *A Casebook in Time-Limited Psychotherapy.* New York: McGraw-Hill.

Reich, W. (1933). *Character Analysis*, trans. T. Wocfus. Rangeley, ME: Orgonics Institute Press.

Ryle, A. (1979). The focus in brief interpretive psychotherapy: dilemmas, traps, and snags. *British Journal of Psychiatry* 134:46–54.

Sach, J. S. (1983). Negative factors in brief psychotherapy: an empirical assessment. *Journal of Consulting and Clinical Psychology* 51:557–564.

Schoenewolf, G. (1993). *Counterresistance: The Therapist's Interference with the Therapeutic Process.* Northvale, NJ: Jason Aronson.

Sifneos, P. E. (1972). *Short-Term Psychotherapy and Emotional Crisis.* Cambridge, MA: Harvard University Press.

——— (1979). *Short-Term Dynamic Psychotherapy: Evaluation and Technique.* New York: Plenum.

Slipp, S. (1993). *Curative Factors in Dynamic Psychotherapy.* Northvale, NJ: Jason Aronson.

Small, L. (1979). *The Briefest Psychotherapies,* 2nd ed. New York: Brunner/Mazel.

Stark, M. (1994). *A Primer on Working with Resistance.* Northvale, NJ: Jason Aronson.

Stierlin, H. (1968). Short-term versus long-term psychotherapy in light of a general theory of human relationships. *British Journal of Psychiatry* 32:127–135.

Wolberg, L. (1980). *Handbook of Short-Term Psychotherapy.* New York: Grune & Stratton.

Zois, C. (1986). Handling resistance in depressed patients. *International Journal of Short-Term Psychotherapy* 1:17–30.

——— (1989). The dynamics of videotaping. *American Psychiatric Association 32, Area II, Council 4.*

——— (1992). *Think Like a Shrink.* New York: Warner Books.

Index

About the Authors

Christ L. Zois, M.D., has been a proponent and teacher of short-term therapy since the early eighties. He was the founder and director of the New York Center for Short-Term Dynamic Psychotherapy and the International Institute of Short-Term Dynamic Psychotherapy. He is a contributor and former member of the editorial board of the *International Journal of Short-Term Psychotherapy*, and has held teaching appointments at Cornell University School of Medicine, New York Medical College, and Albert Einstein College of Medicine. Dr. Zois is the author of *Think Like A Shrink*, a primer on short-term therapy for the layman.

Margaret Scarpa, M.A., C.S.W., is a psychotherapist and a consultant to long-term care facilities. She has held the position of Director of Social Services at two long-term care facilities where she has been involved in creating therapeutic milieus and support services to staff and families.

www.ingramcontent.com/pod-product-compliance
Ingram Content Group UK Ltd.
Pitfield, Milton Keynes, MK11 3LW, UK
UKHW012034150926
475560UK00001B/9

9 780765 70026